TWENTIETH CENTURY INTERPRETATIONS
OF

EURIPIDES'
ALCESTIS

A Collection of Critical Essays

Edited by

JOHN R. WILSON

Prentice-Hall, Inc.  A SPECTRUM BOOK *Englewood Cliffs, N. J.*

Contents

Introduction

by John R. Wilson

Euripides' *Alcestis* has always been a critic's battlefield. Even the genre to which the play belongs is disputed—is it a tragedy, a satyr play, or the first example of a tragicomedy? Who is the main character, Alcestis or Admetus? And through whose eyes are we to see this wife and this husband? Is Alcestis as noble as she says she is? And is Admetus worthy of her devotion, or does he deserve all the blame that his father, Pheres, heaps upon him? And is the salvation of Alcestis a true mystery, a sardonic "and so they lived happily ever after," or simply the convenient end of an entertainment? These are only some of the questions that have been raised about the play, and hardly any of them admit of an unqualified answer.

The author of this problem play was born between 485 and 480 B.C. into a well-to-do Athenian family, but unlike his slightly elder contemporary, Sophocles, he did not engage actively in the life of the city, and is the first Greek author who won a reputation for being bookish. Whether true or not, the story that he spent many solitary hours in a cave on his native Salamis typifies his essential distance and alienation from society.

He first came into prominence in 455, when a tetralogy (a set of three tragedies followed by a satyr play) was accepted for competition in the chief dramatic festival at Athens, the City or Greater Dionysia. As only three tragedians were chosen each year to enter a tetralogy in the festival, the mere privilege of being allowed to compete was already an honor. As a matter of fact, Euripides rarely won the first prize, and in the twenty-two times or so in which he did compete (his total production amounted to about 88 plays) he won the first prize only five times, the fifth being for a posthumous production of a tetralogy which included the *Bacchae* and *Iphigenia at Aulis*. In 408 he left a war-weary Athens to reside at the court of king Archelaos in Macedonia, where he died in the winter of 407-406.

The lack of official approval at Athens did not mean that he was neglected. The tireless attacks of Aristophanes from the comic stage show that he was a deeply disturbing element in the cultural life of the day. In the comedian's mind he was rightly associated with the advanced intellectual milieu of Socrates and other sophists such as Anaxagoras, Prodicus, and Protagoras, who were thought to be subverting the traditional way of life of the old city state or *polis.* Indeed Socrates, though not a theater-goer, was said never to have missed the performance of a work by Euripides.

Euripides' comparative withdrawal from public life and his evident involvement in the open-ended thinking of his age loosened his ties with the community, the *polis,* which traditionally claimed all of a man's allegiance. In 458, while Euripides was still in his twenties, Aeschylus depicted in his crowning work, the *Oresteia,* a grand reconciliation of all discordant and primitive passions and guilts in the clear reasoning atmosphere of Athena's divine city. After that date we find no such resolution of the strains between the individual and society. The tragedian had only two viable courses: either a desperate faith, such as is manifested in that counterpart of the *Oresteia, Oedipus at Colonus,* written by Sophocles at the end of his life when Athens was near destruction and the gulf between the ideal Athens and the real Athens had long since become unbridgeable, or the attitude taken by Euripides in his greatest dramas: simple despair tempered only by protest.

Though historically Euripides lived in a time when the *polis* as an all-absorbing institution was weakening, as a dramatic poet who entered his plays in the Dionysia, he was very much a public figure, and wrote several of his lesser works as frankly patriotic manifestoes. More profoundly, tragedy itself with its largely mythical subject matter, its chorus and set number of actors, its metrical, stylistic, and structural conventions, was itself the repository of a common tradition. Formally, Euripides is a conservative, even an archaizing poet, and it is conceivable that some of his audience accepted his plays in a conventional way. There is, however, a deliberate contrast between the conventional form and the unconventional subject matter, and in his plays we often feel that the form is slightly overlapping the matter. In Sophocles, form and matter make an indissoluble unity, a body, as it were, of faith. Euripides, however, is often a pattern-maker, and stands apart from his creation in a mood of scepticism, disenchantment, or simple virtuosity.

Alcestis, produced in 438, is probably the earliest of the nineteen surviving plays (only *Rhesus,* if it is genuine, is likely to be earlier). It is nevertheless a mature work, written when Euripides was already in his forties and had been publicly recognized as a playwright for seventeen years. It is not surprising then that it is as complex and difficult as any of the plays. What perhaps makes it even more difficult is its prosatyric position. For it was the fourth play in the tetralogy *The Cretan Women, Alcmaeon in Psophis, Telephus, Alcestis,* a position which in all other cases that we know of was occupied by a satyr play. But a true satyr play, such as *Cyclops* (the only complete example of the genre that has survived), is a short, slapstick piece characterized by a chorus of satyrs, half men, half beasts, who are servants of the nature-god Dionysus and who act as a farcical backdrop to the traditional mythological heroes of tragedy. *Alcestis,* in spite of its position, is clearly no such play. It contains no satyrs, and no openly farcical elements, for even the merriment of Heracles is toned down to fit the dignity of a serious drama. It does have a happy ending, but this is quite common in Greek tragedy, which is by no means necessarily 'tragic,' as *Ion, Iphigenia in Tauris,* and *Helen* amply testify. The only elements which may be attributed to its prosatyric function are its relative shortness and its fairy-tale theme, which is unusual, even unique, in extant Greek tragedy.

Formally, *Alcestis* falls into two rather discrete actions which only merge in the final scene. Except for the prologue, the first 475 lines are exclusively concerned with the death and glorification of Alcestis, and this action may be considered in its own right as a miniature tragedy of fate. By her heroic decision she has saved her husband's life, and won herself eternal fame in the process. The entry of Heracles at 476 starts a parallel action in which Admetus also makes an heroic decision: that of playing the perfect host in spite of his wife's death. That the heroic decisions of husband and wife are thought of as parallel is clearly indicated by the language, for both are capable of the same quality of *tolme,* of 'nerve,' usually in the sense of a courageous and decisive commitment. In the ode following Alcestis' death, the chorus, like Admetus later, wish they could bring her up from the dead, "for you were the only one, dearest of women, who had the nerve (*etlas*) to save your husband from death at the cost of your life" (460 f., cf. 624, 741). Those who gave him birth, they go on to say, "did not have the nerve (*etlan*) to save him." In the very next scene Admetus shows his own nerve by receiving Heracles. "What are you doing," exclaims the chorus leader. "Do you have the nerve (*tolmais*) to receive guests in such tragic circumstances? Are you mad?" (551 f.). *Tolme,* in the sense of resolute action, is either criminal or heroic in Greek tragedy. Temporarily, in the case of Admetus, it is thought of as insane. But not for long, for after being enlightened by their monarch, the chorus can see the connection between this extravagant gesture and the previous reception of Apollo into the house, which had had such beneficial results in the past. If being a perfect host had paid off so handsomely then, why shouldn't it do so now? Heracles, too, shows his nerve, at first inadvertently, by celebrating in the midst of grief (752 *etolmese*), but then in a good and consciously heroic way, by summoning up the resolution to save Alcestis. "All daring (*tlasa*) heart and strength of mine, show now the kind of son Alcmene, daughter of Electryon, bore to Zeus" (837 f.).

All three characters, then, are noble through their *tolme* as well as through their birth. Alcestis is repeatedly called *ariste,* best, by the chorus (83, 151, 241, 442, 742), the servant woman (152), Admetus (899), and even by herself (324). The same term is applied by Admetus to Heracles (559), and both men compliment each other on their nobility. "I am sure," says Heracles, "that I will fetch Alcestis from below and place her in the hands of the host who received me in his house and, out of nobility and respect for me, did not turn me away, though he was struck by a cruel misfortune" (853 f.). Heracles is determined to match this nobility, and claims near the end of the play that Admetus will admit when he finds out the identity of the strange woman he brings with him that he has played host to a "noble guest" (1120).

The present-day reader finds no difficulty in appreciating the nobility of Alcestis, or the simple courage of Heracles. But how is Admetus considered worthy of their company? From the mythical point of view, it is precisely the good company he keeps that saves him. In the words of an old, anonymous drinking song:

Hear Admetus' word, friend, and take heed. Choose the good man for thy friend.

Flee from the base, for from the bad, small good you'll get in the end.

(tr. Paul Shorey)

Admetus is *hosios,* punctilious, with the gods, and meets his reward from the punctilious Apollo (10). The pattern is repeated with Heracles, as the chorus admit with unconcealed admiration. And yet his virtue, such as it is, is based on calculations that, though they are familiar to Alcestis and Heracles, are beneath both of them. In his justification for his unexpected hospitality, Admetus does not himself talk about an heroic decision, as Alcestis and Heracles both do, but applies a simple mathematics. He already suffers from the loss of Alcestis, so why add to this the loss of his reputation as a perfect host? This is his answer not only to an incredulous chorus who, to be sure, later interpret his action in an heroic vein, but also to a reproachful Heracles. Why, asks the demi-god, did you mislead me? You can be sure, replies Admetus, it was not to spite you, but only to minimize the unpleasant consequences to myself (only, that is, out of the purest selfishness).

The measurement of pleasure forms the basis of the charge against his father, Pheres, and against his mother. Alcestis puts it very clearly in her final summation before her death. They had little time left to live and little pleasure left to experience, while she could have looked forward to a long life and much pleasure. If Admetus had died, they would have been too old to replace him with another son. Alcestis, on the other hand, could readily have found a new husband (285 f.). The parents might rationally have exchanged the minimal advantage of living longer for the compensation of winning eternal fame. Of course Alcestis, by sacrificing so much, wins an even greater measure of fame, which partially compensates her for the loss of life and pleasure. But in the last analysis she ignores the calculus of pleasure, and through being aware of what she has given up becomes all the more noble. The same may be said of Heracles. Like Admetus, he knows the simple pleasures of archaic man: eating, drinking and making merry while life lasts. But he is aware of the nearness and inevitability of death, and stands ready to lose life, which cannot last long anyway, to win honor. This is the simple nobility about which Sarpedon speaks so memorably to Glaukos in the *Iliad* (12.322 f.):

> Dear friend, if by getting out of this war the two of us were always going to be ageless and deathless, I wouldn't fight in the front rank myself or send you out to win glory in battle. But since the spirits of death hover over us in a thousand shapes, and mankind can neither escape nor duck them, let us go and either give someone else a triumph or triumph for ourselves.

Admetus has no such virtue, but clings to life as though it would last forever.

Admittedly, before Admetus is rewarded for his hospitality by the return of Alcestis, he does partially revise his simplistic philosophy. His initial assumption had been that an extension of life was in itself a blessing. But as Alcestis dies, and particularly after she is dead, he comes to realize that life without her is not pleasurable, i.e., that the privilege of extended life which Apollo gave him is,

after all, without value. Hence, in a speech whose language is suggestive of 'tragic' learning (the "now I understand" of 940 is exactly echoed more than 30 years later in the really tragic "now I
understand" of Agaue at *Bacchae* 1296), he admits that he might
just as well have died himself, for all the good his extended life
does him. His wife is really better off than he is, for now he has to
endure not only loss of comfort but also loss of reputation. Good
fortune and good repute are traditional categories for the measurement of human happiness. Pindar states that "the first thing to
strive for is well-being; the second share is a good reputation: but
whoever happens on both wins the top prize" (*Pythian* I. 99 f.).
Admetus presumably would have been satisfied with well-being
alone, whatever became of his reputation. For in his mind reputation remains something as external and manageable as his original
conception of well-being. But though his conception of well-being
is deepened by his experience into an awareness of spiritual as
well as physical needs, he stoutly refuses to revise his views on
reputation. His ill-repute is merely an unlucky accident which his
enemies take advantage of.

Foremost among his enemies is Pheres. What Admetus imagines
other people saying against him is what Pheres actually says in the
shocking battle of words over a mercifully dead Alcestis. Until this
scene occurs, no word of criticism has been breathed about Admetus'
behavior towards Alcestis. The game is miraculously played as a
tragedy of fate, with Admetus as co-star to his wife. "The sun,"
he says as he first enters the stage with the rapidly failing Alcestis,
"looks upon both of us, a pair in trouble who have done nothing
to the gods to deserve your death" (246 f.). Apollo at the opening,
Alcestis in her final summation, and the chorus everywhere, all
harp on the theme of fatal necessity. In their first appearances, the
chorus are largely concerned with the timing and not at all with
the morality of Alcestis' death. Should they begin mourning for her
now, or wait for later? After she dies they can finally unburden
themselves of a straightforward encomium, in which the only moral
strictures are directed against Admetus' two aged parents, who, as
in Alcestis' own speech, act as a foil to bring out the nobility of
her sacrifice. Later, they turn to Admetus and console him by remarks on the universality of death and the inexorable necessity of
what has happened. Even Pheres, it is important to note, comfort-
ably praises and consoles like everyone else, until he is stung by
Admetus into retaliation. "Everyone will agree that you lost a fine
and sensible wife. It's hard, I realize, but you must bear it. . . ."

He goes on to say that she was a credit to the whole female sex "by having the courage (*tlasa*) to do this noble deed" (624).

But this is only a pious sham. Later on Pheres shows his real thoughts and calls her a fool (728), presumably because she ignored the calculus of pleasure by which both he and his son live. In his stolid insistence on the value of every bit of life left him, he is more than a match for Admetus, who chose to 'kill' his wife in order to save himself, on the assumption that the mere extension of his life was worth it. As Browning remarks, the vitriol of this interchange is partly explained by the fact that the two men know each other too well:

> Like hates like:
> Accordingly Admetos, full i' the face
> Of Pheres, his true father, outward shape
> And inward fashion, body matching soul,
> Saw just himself when years should do their work
> And reinforce the selfishness inside
> Until it pushed the last disguise away:
> As when the liquid metal cools i' the mould,
> Stands forth a statue: bloodless, hard, cold bronze.
> So, in old Pheres, young Admetos showed,
> Pushed to completion: and a shudder ran,
> And his repugnance soon had vent in speech:
> Glad to escape outside, nor, pent within,
> Find itself there fit food for exercise.
>
> (*Balaustion's Adventure,* 1364 f.)

In the Pheres scene, both father and son are revealed in their true light. The father is satisfied with the ugly picture he presents, secure in his well-being and careless of his reputation. The son is more sensitive, cannot be happy in a purely physical way, and is also concerned (however externally) about his reputation. Pheres is personally so discreditable that some are tempted to discount his scathing attack altogether.

Even if we leave this scene out of account, we can see that Admetus betrays Alcestis at every turn. In the scene with Pheres, he passionately disavows his parents (634 f., 666 f.), and states that Alcestis, "a woman outside the family" (i.e., connected by marriage only, and not by blood) will be as mother and father to him. Yet only just before, he has declared to Heracles that she is very much "outside the family" (533), and therefore not entitled to more than perfunctory mourning. As the servant remarks to Heracles, she is "only too much outside it" (811).

Of course Admetus had to deny relationship to the corpse that confronts Heracles in order to carry out what he considered his duties as host, and generally, as we have seen, Heracles takes his sacrifice at face value. But when, after rescuing Alcestis, he meets Admetus for the second time, he expresses a natural feeling that Admetus was not really treating him as a friend when he refused to share his troubles with him. Furthermore, this outrageous denial is only a beginning. In his first encounter with Admetus, Heracles did not know that he was testing which was stronger in his friend, rules of hospitality or attachment to his wife. Now in his second encounter he tests him again, but this time deliberately. Appearing with the unidentified woman, he consciously violates every decency. To begin with, he suggests the possibility of another wife. Admetus stoutly rejects this proposal in a fourfold denial (1090-96), without however mentioning what precludes it in the first place, the promise to never remarry that Alcestis had so insistently extracted from him. Heracles, however, persists in a series of imperatives. At 1101 the stichomythia is dramatically interrupted by a sigh from Admetus, who visibly weakens. (One may compare the similarly dramatic break in the stichomythia at *Bacchae* 810, which marks the point where Pentheus capitulates to Dionysus). The matter is put in agonistic terms: by accepting the woman Admetus will share in Heracles' victory. At 1108 Admetus finally bids Heracles have his way (literally 'have the victory'). Heracles, however, is not content. Admetus must perform one final act of 'daring.' "Have the nerve (*tolma*) to reach out your hand and touch the stranger" (1117). When he does so, he is immediately rewarded with the recognition that "the stranger" is his wife. Thus the two acts of daring, the heroic sacrifice of Alcestis and the heroic hospitality of Admetus result, through the mediation of Heracles, in the miraculous salvation of both.

This final testing of Admetus is reminiscent in an inverse way of a scene in Sophocles' *Electra,* a play written many years later. There Orestes deliberately tests Electra with increasing severity until, when she is at the breaking point, he finally rewards her by identifying himself as the brother whom she thought was dead. He had entered bearing what she imagined to be his ashes in an urn. Before he lets her know his identity, he not only watches her lament over the urn, but also insists that she hand the ashes back to him. Her anguish in doing this reveals the utmost loyalty and we feel that she truly deserves her brother. But when Admetus with a corresponding reluctance accepts the stranger, he is in fact betraying his beloved, and being loyal only to the abstract principles of hospitality. Still, the mounting tension and subsequent relief after recognition is dramatically parallel, and in the final *exeunt omnes* all the characters share in the joy of the occasion without any second thoughts. The simplistic conclusion is that Admetus should continue in his hospitable endeavors (1148).

But there is another more sinister parallel to this scene. When, in the carpet scene of *Agamemnon*, Clytaemestra asserts her will over her husband, she and her husband talk in the same agonistic terms as Heracles and Admetus. Like Heracles, Clytaemestra wins a "victory" over her opponent, and as in *Alcestis* the whole scene fatally re-enacts an original weakness of will on the part of the defeated. Agamemnon gracefully gives in to his wife and walks on the purple carpet, thus repeating in a symbolic way his former error at Calchis, just as Admetus gracefully gives in to Heracles, and repeats his former betrayal before the corpse of his wife.

The ending of the play, with its bland assumption that 'all's well that ends well,' is the first, as Kurt von Fritz has shown (*see* p. 80), in a series of bitter-sweet happy endings which culminate in the shockingly immoral ending of *Orestes*. But in *Alcestis* the tone is tolerant and amused. After all, Admetus is somewhat endearing in his incorrigible obtuseness. In different circumstances, as von Fritz observes,[1] he might have developed the ugliness of a Jason, who somewhat resembles him in blandly assuming the privileges he considers due to his class and sex. But Admetus, in sharp contrast to Jason, is strangely romantic in his feelings for his wife. He will always grieve for her, and will solace his passion by embracing a facsimile of her, just as in Euripides' *Protesilaos* Laodameia, in grief over the loss of her newly wedded husband, makes a likeness of him and keeps it in her bedroom. Admetus' extravagance about the statue is followed by his comparison to Orpheus: like him, he would descend into the underworld to fetch his beloved—would, if only he could. But at least he will eventually lie side by side with her in death. This passion is not entirely rhetorical, for after her death he actually attempts to throw himself into the grave to join her, and reproaches the chorus for not letting him do it. "Hades would have had two souls instead of one, a most devoted pair, who would have crossed the underworld lake together" (900 f.). Here and elsewhere in the play Admetus assumes the romantic sentiments

[1] *Antike und Moderne Tragödie* (Berlin, 1962), pp. 347, 358.

that readers often attribute to Alcestis, who is in fact decidedly un-romantic.

Admetus ignores the unpleasant truth presented to him by Pheres, but in this he shares the attitude of the chorus and of Alcestis herself. Alcestis wishes that Admetus' parents had had the decency to make the necessary sacrifice and let her and Admetus live out their natural lives together. But, as she puts it, fate would have it differently (there is no word here of Admetus). The chorus constantly wishes for a softening of this inflexible fate, and as Admetus refers to Orpheus, who could bring back Eurydice, so they refer to the divine healer Asclepius, who was able to do the impossible and raise the dead (122 f.). Asclepius is the child of Apollo, and it is to Apollo that they turn in their final appeal before the death scene (220 f.). In a typical form of Greek prayer, they remind him of his previous favor in cheating death, and ask him to repeat the miracle. Of course, they don't believe that this is possible, and they end each excursion into wishful thinking on a note of helplessness.[2] As the maid remarks, Admetus, when he tearfully implores his dying wife not to 'betray' him, is "after the impossible" (202 f.). But in terms of the plot the choral prayer to Apollo is fully answered, and the most extravagant wishes of all are fully realized. Alcestis does not in the end 'betray' Admetus, and the perfect pair are reunited.

If we ask how the play's romantic and satiric strains unite, we are left, I think, with a paradox. From one point of view the passion of Admetus is intolerable. It is all very well, for example, that Theseus in *Hippolytus* should beg his dying son not to 'betray' him (1454), for he has not deliberately caused his death. It is scandalous in the case of Admetus. Yet everyone except the disgusting Pheres connives in supporting him, and the romantic emotions he feeds on are real enough, even though not based on reality. In a sense the plot works against Admetus, for, as we have seen, the assertion of his heroic hospitality (in fact only self-interest even from Admetus' point of view) involves the betrayal of his wife, and this is reinforced in the temptation scene at the end. Yet the same scene which caps the ironical treatment of Admetus' virtues is also the conclusion of a fairy tale in which the powers of light, notably Apollo, defeat the powers of darkness and death. This conflict has its own structural pattern which is in counterpoint to the ironical structure. The bright Apollo faces off against the sulky Thanatos in the prologue. For the next part of the play Thanatos reigns supreme, and life is

---

[2] 231 f., cf. 455 f. and especially 962 f., where Apollo and Orpheus are both mentioned as helpless against the force of Necessity.

only spoken of as a wish for the impossible. But then, when the jovial Heracles arrives, life and death are once more sharply juxtaposed, especially in the description of how Heracles' raucous revelling clashes with the sounds of lamentation (760 f.). Heracles, as Apollo had predicted, sets moving a counterplot which will bring about the triumph over death, and when he discovers the cause for lamentation, he immediately goes to rescue Alcestis. But before he returns, the tragic plot is further intensified by the despair of Admetus as he comes back from the funeral and by the climactic ode on Necessity (a generalization of Death). This ode is immediately followed by the entry of Heracles, who brings Alcestis with him and is triumphant over that same Necessity. The interweaving of plot and counterplot now finds a happily unreal solution which is only bitter when measured against the moral reality which nearly everyone conspires to forget.

No wonder, then, that *Alcestis* has met with such diverse interpretations. Euripides plays with virtuosity on an archaic set of assumptions which are first rudely shattered by Pheres and then blithely assumed to have remained intact. This double-take produces both a romantic drama and a wicked satire. An added complication is that Alcestis herself stands a little apart from both the romance and the satire. She looks forward to those other heroines Makaria in the *Heracleidae,* Polyxena in *Hekabe,* and Iphigenia in *Iphigenia at Aulis,* all of whom show the same brittle purity of self-sacrifice. Indeed the silence of Alcestis in the final scene has an artistic as well as a ritual motivation, for through it she neatly dissociates herself from the unreal world around her, in which Admetus and the others can have their cake and eat it too.

Euripides was apparently the first to make a problem play out of the myth. In the folk-tale analogues (explored notably by Albin Lesky[3]) the beneficiary of the sacrifice is just an object—never considered in his or her own right—and the point lies only in the nobility of the sacrifice itself. In all stories either the wife or (in Germanic versions) the lover makes the sacrifice when the parents hold back. The attitude is one of uncomplicated admiration, as in Plato's reference to the myth (*Symposium* 179B):

> Furthermore, only lovers are willing to die for another. This is true of women as well as men. In the Greek world adequate proof is provided by Alcestis, the daughter of Pelias, who was the only one

[3] *Alkestis, der Mythus und das Drama:* SB. Wiener Ak., ph.-hist. Kl. CCIII, 2, Vienna 1925.

willing to die for her husband, even though his father and mother
were alive. The ties of love made her so superior to them that she
showed them up as being strangers to their son and only technically
related. . . .

More likely than not the only other attested treatment in Greek
tragedy of the Alcestis story, that of Phrynichus (an older contemporary of Aeschylus), did not raise any ethical problems either, except of course the simple one of the parents' cowardice *vs.* the wife's
bravery.

Later treatments of the theme in European literature all take
Euripides' *Alcestis* as a model, and all of them emasculate it. The
general tendency is to rescue Admetus by making him unaware of
the choice that is presented to those around him. Once he learns
about it, Alcestis has already made her sacrifice and it is too late.
Such is the situation in Calzabigi's libretto to Gluck's opera (1767),
and also in Wieland's Singspiel (1773), which in his own estimation
was a great improvement on the Euripidean original (such self-
assurance prompted the youthful Goethe to write his spoof *Götter,
Helden, und Wieland* the following year). Wieland depicts Admetus
and Alcestis in a competition of self-sacrifice. In such a conflict between "the good and the better" there is no room for Pheres, though
in a version by Alfieri (1798) Pheres and Admetus compete in
nobility even before Admetus is aware of the situation. In a "free
translation" of Euripides' play (1898), Hugo von Hofmannsthal
adopts the bizarre expedient of having Admetus freely accept the
sacrifice in his capacity as king: he is the indispensable ruler, whose
survival is necessary for the well-being of his subjects. More interesting is Robert Browning's *Balaustion's Adventure* (1871), which
includes a fairly accurate version of the Euripidean text, but inter-
lards it with Balaustion's own psychologizing comments. Balaustion
makes no attempt to whitewash Admetus, but shows what she considers to be his gradual rehabilitation. After she has recited Euripides' play, however, Balaustion feels impelled to add a version of
her own in which Admetus and Alcestis are equally heroic and
equally unreal.

The most important work of recent literature based on *Alcestis*
is Eliot's *The Cocktail Party* (1950), which transmutes an essentially
Browningesque interpretation of Euripides' play (Edward, like
Browning's Admetus, moves steadily to redemption) into a Christian
morality play. But the transmutation is so radical that it can hardly
be called a treatment of the Alcestis myth. Indeed Eliot had to be
his own detective in this and point out his model to the critics.

Furthermore, despite the ingenuities of Eliot's treatment, I would agree with Arrowsmith[4] that his split between the secular and the sacred is not adequately grounded in the poetry itself. Euripides is far more honest, and in fact gives the devil his due to such an extent that he is still misinterpreted through the simplification of an exclusively romantic approach. In its technically brilliant fusion of romanticism, with its wish for the impossible; of satire, with its dissection of conventional values; and of true heroism in the person of Alcestis, Euripides gives the play a disturbing quality which, as in so many of his works, still challenges the honesty of our response.

[4] In the last part of the essay "The Comedy of T. S. Eliot" whose opening pages are reprinted here under the title " 'Conversion' in Euripides," p. 31.

PART ONE

Interpretations

The Myth and Its Adaptation

by D. J. Conacher

In an attempt to judge the nature and purpose of Euripides' treatment of the myths of Admetus and Alcestis, let us set down the bare
events as Euripides gives them, together with what we know of this
material from other sources.

Apollo tells us in the prologue of the *Alcestis* that he had enabled
King Admetus to postpone his impending death by persuading the
Fates to let Admetus off if he could find someone willing to die in
his place; this sacrifice Alcestis, wife of Admetus, has accepted after
both his parents had refused it, and now the appointed day for
Alcestis' death is at hand. Apollo explains as follows his own involvement with Admetus: furious at the death of his son Asclepius,
slain by Zeus' thunderbolt, Apollo had in turn slain the Cyclopes
(makers of thunderbolts) and for punishment had been enslaved for
a period to the mortal Admetus; it was during this sojourn that the
threat to Admetus' life occurred and Apollo intervened, in gratitude
for his human master's piety toward him.

After this monologue, Thanatos (Death) appears, to begin his
fell office. After further unsuccessful attempts to dissuade him,
Apollo prophesies that Heracles (identified by description rather
than by name) will wrest Alcestis by force from Thanatos. In the
course of the play, Alcestis dies, but not before her husband has
promised her, in gratitude, a life of celibacy for himself and of
cheerless mourning for himself and his house. During the funeral
arrangements, Heracles visits Admetus' palace and, unaware of the
situation, is hospitably entertained by Admetus; when he learns of

"The Myth and Its Adaptation" by D. J. Conacher. From Euripidean Drama,
Myth, Theme and Structure (*Toronto: University of Toronto Press, 1967*), *pp.
327-33. Copyright 1967 by University of Toronto Press and Oxford University
Press. Reprinted by permission of the author and publishers.*

14

his host's hospitable dissimulation, he rewards it by overcoming Thanatos in an off-stage wrestling match and restoring Alcestis to Admetus.

Even at first glance, a certain cleavage, a certain basic lack of congeniality, appears between different elements in this myth. On the one hand, we have an Olympian, Apollo, and his relations with a human hero, King Admetus; on the other hand, we have Thanatos, a creature of folk-tale, carrying off the King's .wife who is, in turn, rescued by a sort of superman, Heracles. The only connection which Apollo has with the action of the play itself is that he first arranges the "privilege" of the substitute death; after a brief attempt to put off Thanatos, Apollo leaves the scene for good, and the final over-coming of death is effected in a manner quite alien to the mythical world which Apollo inhabits.

This initial impression of cleavage increases greatly when we look at the mythological tradition relevant to the play. There is evidence of early accounts of Apollo's bondage to Admetus (e.g., a passing reference in Homer, signs of a fuller account in the Hesiodic cata-logue)[1] but no actual mention, before tragedy, of Alcestis' self-sacrifice. This does not, of course, mean that the Alcestis legend did not exist before then, but it may indicate that it was not always attached to the Apollo-Admetus story and that, consequently, it was not always a part of the main mythical tradition. The only known treatment of the Alcestis theme itself before Euripides is that of Phrynichus' *Alcestis*[2] of which we have only one actual quotation:

σῶμα δ' ἀθαμβὲς† γυοδόνιστον† τείρει
He constrains the fearless, limb-driven [?] (limb-mastered [?]) body.

(frg. 2)

This fragment is usually taken, though with no certainty, to refer to the wrestling match between Heracles and Thanatos. It is possible that Aeschylus' reference (*Eumenides*, 723-28) to Apollo's persuasion

---

[1] There seems to be an oblique reference to Apollo's bondage to Admetus, son of Pheres, at *Il.* 2. 763-66; Homer's only reference to Alcestis with Admetus occurs in his naming of the parents of Eumelus at *Il.* 2. 713-15. For the Hesiodic references, see Hesiod, fragments 122-27 (Rzach) from the *Ehoiai*, or *Catalogue of Famous Women*. A scholium to Euripides, *Alc.* 1 (Hes. frg. 127) assures us that in the parts of the myth concerning Apollo's enslavement to Admetus, Euripides is following the common tale as told by Hesiod and Asclepiades. (The scholiast also adds several other ancient sources, including writers as early as Stesichorus and Pherecydes, for this part of the myth.)

[2] See Nauck, *TGF*, p. 720.

of the Moirai, by drink, to spare men's lives, and the Euripidean
Apollo's casual reference to his tricking of the Fates (*Alcestis,* 12),
may be allusions to Phrynichus' treatment of the theme. (If so, one
is tempted to think Phrynichus' *Alcestis* must have been a satyr-
play.) Apart from this, all we know of the lost play is that Thanatos
appeared in it carrying a sword for the ritual cutting of Alcestis'
hair. (frg. 3)

The "Hesiodic" account seems to have been concerned entirely
with the background of Apollo's bondage to Admetus: Apollo's
jealous vengeance, with Artemis' help, on his beloved and unfaithful
Coronis; his saving of Asclepius, his son by Coronis, Zeus' blasting
of Asclepius for raising men from the dead; Apollo's reprisals against
the Cyclopes (the makers of Zeus' thunderbolts) and his subsequent
enslavement to Admetus in punishment. Only the last of these details is factually relevant to Euripides' plot, though there is a certain
thematic overlap in the roles of Asclepius and Heracles.

Among the post-Classical accounts of the Apollo-Admetus-Alcestis
myths, that of Apollodorus is of the greatest interest. Here it is worth
noting that the myth ending with Apollo's enslavement to Admetus
is told separately from the Admetus-Alcestis legend.[3] The former
follows very closely the main lines of the early ("Hesiodic") version,
while the Admetus-Alcestis legend differs in several respects from
Euripides' version. The latter account runs as follows:

> When Admetus reigned over Pherae, Apollo served him as his thrall,
> while Admetus wooed Alcestis, daughter of Pelias. Now Pelias had
> promised to give his daughter to him who should yoke a lion and a
> boar to a car, and Apollo yoked them and gave them to Admetus,
> who brought them to Pelias and so obtained Alcestis. But in offering
> a sacrifice at his marriage, he forgot to sacrifice to Artemis; therefore
> when he opened the marriage chamber, he found it full of coiled
> snakes. Apollo bade him appease the goddess and obtained as a favour
> of the Fates that, when Admetus should be about to die, he might be
> released from death if someone should choose voluntarily to die for
> him. And when the day of his death came neither his father nor his
> mother would die for him, but Alcestis died in his stead. But the
> Maiden [Persephone] sent her up again, or, as some say, Hercules
> fought with Hades [and brought her up to him]. [The last clause is
> omitted in the MSS.]

Here the most interesting differences from the Euripidean version
are: the role of Artemis and the alternative explanations of the

---

[3] See Apollodorus, *Bibl.* 3. 10. 3-4 and 1. 9. 15 respectively. The translation of
the latter passage, quoted below, is that of Sir James Frazer.

restoration of Alcestis. The anger of Artemis perhaps explains the unexplained "imminent death" mentioned as threatening Admetus in Euripides' version (*Alc.* 13), though there seems to be an interesting hint of a *non sequitur* in Apollodorus between the "appeasing of Artemis" and the favour obtained from the Fates. The peaceful version of Alcestis' return to life is, of course, the one more favourable to the gods of mythology (one should note, by the way, that Hades has been substituted for Thanatos even in the other version) and it is this version too which Plato follows (*Symposium* 179b 5 ff.), when he tells us that the gods returned Alcestis of their own accord in admiration of her deed. Robert suggests that Plato himself may have invented this milder version; however this may be, we may accept his view that the more violent version is the older one.[4]

It seems clear from all that has been said that the myth leading to the enslavement of Apollo to Admetus and the myth involving Alcestis' "substitute" death for Admetus were originally of quite separate and indeed fundamentally different origins. The former belongs to the anthropomorphic and essentially literary tradition of Olympian mythology; the latter, with its bargains and struggles with the monster Thanatos, that pathetically simple incarnation of human fears, suggests the primitive, superstitious and infinitely more urgent preoccupations of folk tale—until, of course, it becomes softened by late and artificial mythologizing. Indeed it is not until Hyginus (*Fab.* 49 and 51), in the second century A.D., and Zenobius (1. 18) that we find a continuous narrative starting from the myths of Apollo and Asclepius and ending with the death and restoration of Alcestis. Despite all contrary indications, Wilamowitz, followed by Ebeling, Séchan, Méridier and others, argues that this *consecutive* treatment found in the late writers goes back to the "canonical" formulation of the Hesiodic catalogue, which he also claims to be the source of the two accounts in Apollodorus; this view has been rightly rejected by Professor A. Lesky and Miss A. M. Dale.[5]

In default of evidence establishing the literary ancestry of the Alcestis theme prior to Greek tragedy, let us turn to the "arguments from probability" by which Robert, Lesky and others assert that the core of our story belongs to popular folk tale rather than to literary

---

[4] C. Robert, *Thanatos* (Berlin 1879), 29-30.

[5] See U. von Wilamowitz, *Philol. Untersuchungen*, IX, 68 ff. and (on the alleged origins and significance of such popular religious poetry attributed to Hesiod), *Griechische Tragoedien*, III, 7 ff., in Wilamowitz's introduction to *Alkestis*. Cf. also Méridier, in his introduction to *Alcestis*, in *Euripide*, I, 46-47 and (in contrast) A. M. Dale, *Euripides, Alcestis*, ix.

tradition. The most ambitious attempt to establish the actual folk-tale kernel of the Alcestis myth has been made by Lesky who, after discussing the relation of popular to literary mythology in general, outlines three European folk tales, preserved in German, Greek and Armenian folk songs, which contain elements of the basic situation in the *Alcestis*.[6] Stripping these songs of their individual developments and variations, Lesky reduces the story to what he considers to be its simplest and oldest form: On the wedding day of a King, Death comes for the bridegroom; Death is willing to accept a substitute, but both the King's parents refuse the sacrifice; finally, the young bride intervenes and follows Death to save the life of her beloved.[7]

Lesky lists several variations and developments: husband dies for doomed bride (manly German version as opposed to eastern expressions of female inferiority!); a physical struggle with Death as well as (originally instead of?) a substitute death, and so on. *Whenever the physical struggle with Death is introduced, the husband himself is the challenger, and when, for one reason or another, he fails, his life is saved only by the self-sacrifice of his bride.*

It is interesting to contrast the way in which this duplication of methods for dealing with Death is handled in Euripides' play. Here, one device is used to save the husband, the other, his self-sacrificing wife. Moreover, in our *Alcestis*, the dramatist further separates the two devices (and so uses them to better effect) by attaching one of them to the mythical, "divine" prologue (where Apollo tells of persuading the Fates to accept Alcestis as a substitute), while reserving the other for the "folk-tale" *dénouement*, where a hero struggles with the primitive figure of Thanatos. Finally, in Euripides' version, the hero who struggles with Death is an outside agent, not, as in the folk songs, the husband himself. Thus, while both ways of foiling Death are presented, the husband engages in neither while gaining from both. Already we catch a glimpse of a whole new dimension, full of psychological and ethical possibilities, in Euripides' adaptation.

How did such a folk tale come to be attached to the end of a myth dealing with the enslavement of Apollo? Nobody knows, of course, but there have been some interesting guesses. Carl Robert points to

[6] A. Lesky, *Alkestis: Der Mythus und das Drama.* The German, Greek and Armenian folk songs are outlined and discussed at pp. 20 ff., 27 ff., and 30 ff., respectively. Cf. also Christ-Schmid, I, 355-56, n. 1, where the folk-tale aspects of Euripides' *Alcestis* are also stressed.

[7] This is a paraphrase of the summary in Lesky, 41-42; cf. *ibid.*, 36-41.

Euripides' own words at *Alcestis* 445 ff. (where the Chorus prophesies that the Queen's fame will be celebrated in song at Sparta at the time of the Carnean festival, as well as at Athens) and suggests that it was at the Carnea, which honoured Apollo, and at similar popular celebrations of Apollo at Athens, that the simple folk song got its poetic development.[8] However, this still does not explain why it became attached to the Apollo myth in the first place. Thessaly, a region much given to chthonian cults, was surely a congenial place for such a folk tale to be developed, and Admetus, to whom Apollo was enslaved, was a Thessalian king. Other scholars go rather further in this matter and point to connections between Admetus and *Hades adamastos* ("the unconquerable") and between "Admetus the hospitable" and *Hades poludegmon, Hades poluxenos!*[9] There are other possible links between the Apollo myth and the Alcestis story: Asclepius, Apollo's son, is the hero who, foreshadowing Heracles' role in our play, raised men from the dead, and Apollo himself is, of course, the Olympian opponent *par excellence* of the chthonic powers. In this connection, Aeschylus' reference (*Eumenides,* 723 ff.) to Apollo's cheating of the Fates in Admetus' interest is most suggestive, for it is in the *Eumenides* that we have the greatest literary expression of this aspect of Apollo.

In Euripides' *Alcestis,* we have two interventions from "outside," one by Apollo before the action of the play begins, and one by Heracles at its conclusion. Obviously, no one like Heracles was needed in the original folk tale: as we have seen, any Death-wrestling that was to be done was done by the husband himself. Nor does Heracles have any part in the Apollo myth. When did he come into the picture?

The possibility that Euripides himself first introduced the role of Heracles into the Alcestis myth has been raised by one or two scholars, most notably Ebeling, though his approach is very different from the one which we have been following.[10] It is true that this suggestion contradicts the view (rather uncertainly based on Phrynichus, fr. 1) that Euripides followed Phrynichus' *Alcestis* in this matter. Ebeling's argument that Phrynichus' play could hardly have

---

[8] Robert, 29.

[9] For a sympathetic summary of such views, see L. Séchan, "Le Dévouement d'Alceste," I, 490-514, esp. 493-98, and references to Wilamowitz and Bloch there given.

[10] See Herman L. Ebeling, *TAPA,* XXIX, 65-85, esp. 74-77. Cf. also Th. Bergk, *Griechische Literaturgeschichte,* III, 498, who believes that in Phrynichus' *Alcestis,* Alcestis' return was the gift of the gods of the Underworld.

extended from Apollo's outwitting of the Fates (see Aeschylus, *Eumenides* 723-28) to the rescue of Alcestis by Heracles, seems weak. Euripides himself "covers" this much, if we include what Apollo tells us in the prologue—and not much more than this would be needed to explain the (quite hypothetical) reference to Phrynichus' play in Aeschylus' *Eumenides*. It seems preferable to point out that no opinion concerning the content of Phrynichus' *Alcestis* can really be based on a tiny fragment in which text, meaning, reference and context are all uncertain.[11]

Ebeling's suggestion that the role of Heracles is Euripides' invention fits well with what he, in common with several recent critics, feels to be an important aspect of Euripides' treatment: the new kind of emphasis on the role of Admetus.[12] It has not, perhaps, been generally recognized that this emphasis depends in large part on Heracles, for without the intrusion of that hero it would not have been easy to present the "restoration" of Alcestis as in some way related to the character and actions of Admetus. Indeed, without Heracles, very little in the way of decisive action would have been left for Admetus at all.

In the folk tale, no one ever wins the wrestling match with Death; nor would the somewhat sentimental "moral" ending which Plato chose have suited the sinister figure of Death in Euripides' piece. To achieve a happy ending within the chosen ethos a typically Euripidean rescuer must be imported—and in a pro-satyric play, what figure could be more suitable than Heracles? Throughout Euripides' work, we find him the most inventive of the dramatists, and the more remote his material, the more daring his innovations. The present device, the appearance of an unexpected rescuer from outside the immediate context of the legendary situation or (sometimes) of the poet's own plot, occurs in one form or another in the *Medea*, the *Heracles* and the *Andromache*, and in at least two of these instances, the "intrusion" appears to have been a Euripidean innovation in the legend concerned.

Finally, the motivation of Heracles' role provides a nice, ironical balance to the mythological introduction to the theme, and one consistent with Euripides' derogatory treatment of the Olympians, particularly of Apollo. The god, in saving his hospitable host Admetus, has placed Alcestis in her present plight and has proved unable to

[11] On this fragment of Phrynichus, cf. also Dale, xiii-xiv, and references there given.

[12] See Ebeling, 65-66, 76-77.

extricate her; now the hero Heracles, also in gratitude for Admetus'
hospitality, succeeds by his "folk-tale methods" in doing what Apollo
has tried and failed to do.[13]

[13] The suggestion that Euripides introduced Heracles into the Alcestis story
must, of course, remain conjectural. It should be added, however, that there
appears to be no evidence in painting or sculpture to contradict either this view
or the view previously expressed concerning the relatively late entry of the theme
of Alcestis' self-sacrifice into the main tradition of Greek mythology. According
to J. A. Paton, *AJA*, IV, 150-51, "The myth was not popular in the earlier art
and no unquestioned representations of it have survived." J. D. Beazley, *Etruscan
Vase Paintings*, 134, refers to but one uncertain representation of Alcestis on an
Attic neck amphora (Louvre F60). The fourth-century Etruscan representations
of the Alcestis story do not include the figure of Heracles.

Greek Tragicomedy

by Hazel E. Barnes

It is a commonplace observation that the tragic and the comic, like all extremes, tend to pass into one another. This happens not because they are basically the same, but because they derive from radically different attitudes toward a single object. Both the tragic and comic points of view are necessarily one-sided—as any angle of vision must be—but they present themselves always as total. If pushed too far, their partiality becomes obvious, and the viewer feels the necessity of recognizing the possibility of another perspective.

Then what of the tragicomic? Is this a new view entirely? Is it merely an uncertain focus? Or does it somehow achieve the feat of maintaining side by side the separate visions of our two eyes?

Obviously, if I am to speak meaningfully of tragicomedy, I must first define my own position with respect to the nature of the tragic and comic attitudes and their object. It is evident that at the origin of all dramatic conflict, there is the fact of the discrepancy between man's aspirations, or pretensions, and his achievement. Whether overtly universal or ostensibly concerned solely with particular struggles, any work of art explicitly or implicitly makes a judgment on the human condition as such. Tragedy and comedy represent two reactions to its ambiguity. Possibly we need not go so far as Schopenhauer and conclude that every individual life is a tragedy when seen from the point of view of the whole and a comedy if examined in its details.[1] Still we must acknowledge that man's imaginative reach transcends his actual capabilities. The goal he attains is never quite the same as the one he projects. By his acts he inscribes himself in a world which he can never fully control, which

---

[1] Arthur Schopenhauer, *The world as will and idea,* 4. 58.

distorts and disappoints his projects, which he cannot comprehend
any more than he can understand himself. Each person is a self-
creation, but chance furnishes most of the material out of which he
must make himself. In short, man is absurd, but he does not always
find his situation laughable.

In tragedy man never gives up the claim that things ought to be
different and that no amount of *species aeternitatis* can unstain
black to white. And it all matters. If Aristotle's statement that
tragedy makes men better than they are means anything, it means
that they are portrayed as more significant, more signifying. Tragedy
is a revolt. No matter what he finds the Universe to be, or his own
particular life, man refuses to deny his aspirations. He will discover
or invent a meaning which allows purpose and dignity in his existence, or he will proclaim loudly that he will never leave off asserting
that it ought to be there. Tragedy is, as well, an affirmation of the
individual man. It moves away from the norm. Tragedy is Christian
in its assertion of the infinite value of every soul, non-Christian in
that it lacks full faith in the over-all rightness of things.

Here I should dispel two possible misunderstandings, even though
the first of these is barely germane to my discussion. First, I do not
agree with those critics who deny the possibility of Christian tragedy.[2] They argue that the promise of eternal bliss cancels out for
the believer any sacrifice he may make, beatifies and erases all
suffering. On the other hand, they say, a person who rejects salvation
is too obviously and stupidly wrong to win our sympathy as a tragic
hero. This thesis seems to me to miss the point entirely. True
Christian tragedy proposes a choice as hopeless as Antigone's. Its
hero faces the necessity of asserting himself as man, thus facing
eternal damnation, or choosing paradise at the expense of all those
claims which make him uniquely human and himself. The choice
between glorifying one's creative potentialities as creature or returning submissively to the hand of the Creator represents the
height of tragic dilemma.

Second, someone might object that Aeschylus' *Oresteia,* for example, is based precisely on the concept that the Universe is just
and rational and that the acquittal of Orestes is the final proof. True,
if one considers only the philosophical resolution at the end. But
we must judge the effect of the trilogy as a whole. Otherwise we fall
into the trap of assuming that tragedy is characterized simply by its

[2] I am thinking particularly here of D. D. Raphael's *The paradox of tragedy*
and of relevant sections in Walter Kaufmann's *Critique of religion and philosophy* and *From Shakespeare to Existentialism.*

unhappy ending. Greek drama in particular often concludes with a denouement insuring that for the still living characters the immediate problem has been successfully resolved. Yet I do not believe that anyone would for this reason call such a work as the *Oresteia* a comedy or even a suspense drama. A tragedy may affirm at its close that justice or love ultimately conquers, or that the grandeur of humanity in suffering is itself a triumph; the exalted finale does not wipe out the absolute evil which has gone before. Orestes vindicated does not justify a world in which Agamemnon, Clytemnestra, Iphigeneia, and the others have done wrong and suffered. The price is too high. There is, in the Universe of tragedy, an Original Sin which no artistic Grace can wash away.

Where tragedy is "twice born," comedy is for the "once born." It calls us back to the comfortable norm. It may satirically attack individuals or institutions, but they are regarded as temporary aberrations from the clear path of common sense, always open to correction. Comedy plays for laughs the absurdity of a creature who mistakenly thinks now that he is simply an automaton, now that he is pure controlling spirit, whereas in truth he is wholly neither and partly both.[3] Comedy scoffs at aspirations for what cannot be. It glorifies the average—without heroics. Superficially it is more optimistic concerning the chances of human happiness. Yet there is a genuine question whether the comic view is really more or less cynical, hopeful, or realistic than the tragic. Comedy "accepts the Universe," but it settles for less.

Tragicomedy, though harder to define, is not merely a convenient term to apply when one is not sure whether the playwright meant his play to be viewed as tragic or comic. Two distinctions should be made at the start. First, there is a difference between the deliberately tragicomic and that merging or juxtaposition of tragic and comic which happens accidentally. If an unskilled actor mismanages Cassandra's ὀτοτοτοτοῖ πόποι δᾶ, the audience may find it ridiculous without thereby losing the sense of tragedy in the scene which follows. There is no true tragicomedy here, rather a brief intrusion of the comic and an artistic failure.

Second, we should probably distinguish between the tragicomic and tragicomedy. The tragicomic may be momentary, fleeting; it is usually confined at most to a single scene. Thus in *The Mikado,* Katisha is unmistakably a comic heroine, but the quality of her

---

[3] I acknowledge a general indebtedness to Bergson and to Meredith, though I have not borrowed directly from either and would not be in total agreement with either.

song "Hearts do not break" introduces something somber. Her appearance and ridiculous behavior preclude the tragic sense, but there is a revelation of the subjective side of her sadness which temporarily checks our laughter. Katisha is funny, but a broken heart is not.

Tragicomic moments in comedy may occur, as with Katisha, when we suddenly see an amusing character from the inside. Or they may result from the fact that in the middle of a foolish plot, our sympathy or admiration for a particular hero or heroine leads us to take his suffering seriously. Apparently Greek New Comedy was full of such scenes. One instance, from Menander's *Arbitration,* is Pamphila's declaration of loyalty to the husband who so inexplicably mistreats her. Alcmena in Plautus' *Amphitryon* and Tyndarus in *The Captives* are comparable characters.

An example of the tragicomic from Greek tragedy is Iolaus' would-be rejuvenation in Euripides' *Children of Heracles.* The old man is both comic and pathetic as he insists on arming himself and starting off to battle. Even if we were tempted to see him as heroic, Euripides has given the attendant lines which forbid us to do so. Typical is this passage (680-90):

Iolaus. And I'll fight with you. Obviously we agree that we must stand by our friends and help them.
Attendant. It's not right for you to talk like a fool.
Iolaus. It's not right for me not to share in a brave fight, along with my friends.
Attendant. Looks won't wound anyone if the arm can't move!
Iolaus. What? Wouldn't I be strong enough to cut through a shield?
Attendant. You'd have the strength, but you'd fall down first yourself.
Iolaus. There isn't one of my enemies will dare to look me in the face!
Attendant. My friend, your strength is no longer what it used to be.
Iolaus. I will fight with just as many as I ever did.
Attendant. It will be a small weight that you add to the scale for your friends!

Iolaus' unrealistic aspirations evoke laughter as well as pity and fear. Neither the tragic nor the comic attitude can quite exclude its opposite.

A second tragicomic scene occurs in Euripides' *Andromache,* where Hermione and Andromache insult each other's sexual appetites and capacities and family backgrounds, accompanied by the chorus' dry commentary, "There's always a tinge of jealousy in the female temperament, and it's downright hostile in the case of rival wives" (181-2). The dialogue is extremely funny, but Andromache's situation is too desperate, her words too bitterly true, for us to laugh it all off as pure comedy.

Both of these scenes may properly be called tragicomic, but they do not make the dramas which contain them tragicomedies, even though in both instances the characters who give the plays their titles finally triumph. In *Andromache,* Thetis' comforting words to Peleus cannot restore Pyrrhus to life. In the *Children of Heracles,* the scene with Iolaus was preceded by the moving self-sacrifice of Macaria. The play's conclusion, despite the tale of Iolaus' heroism and Alcmene's rejoicing at the capture of Eurystheus, is intensely tragic. Alcmene, by her decision to have her enemy killed, disobeys Athens, which has generously defended her. Ingratitude is also betrayal, for Eurystheus' prophecy, which Alcmene disregards, foretells that the descendants of the Heraclidae will one day come to attack Athens.

A tragicomedy is a deliberate creation. It is not an artistic failure except in the mind of the Procrustean critic who insists on reading it as if it were intended to be typical tragedy or comedy. Nor is it merely a play which happens to contain both grave suffering and humor. If we are to call a drama a tragicomedy, this must be because it exhibits in its total structure and treatment a point of view that is demonstrably distinct from both comedy and tragedy. The color of tragicomedy is less pure, even a mixture perhaps, but it is definitely itself, just as a fabric displaying black polka dots on a white background is recognizably different from either straight black or straight white.

Tragicomedy, as a literary form, develops from or involves one or more of three dramatic situations: (1) a disproportion between the content as it is normally judged and the attitude toward it which is induced by the behavior of the characters and the overall dramatic style; (2) an unrealistic closing up or denial of the gap between desire and reality, what I would call a betrayal of the human condition; (3) a discrepancy between the attitude of the characters and that of the spectators—not as the result of "tragic irony" but when all the facts are in.

In Greek literature, true tragicomedy seems to me to be found only in the work of Euripides, in the group of plays which uneasy scholars have variously labeled melodrama, romances, anticipations of New Comedy, or substitutes for the satyr play. In principle I agree that it is better not to attempt to classify all fiction as tragedy, comedy, or tragicomedy. There are other genres, the suspense tale, the detective story, historical and science fiction, all of which, more often than not, involve chiefly the posing and solving of a problem. Possibly there is some of Euripides which should be relegated to such a category. I myself should not object to so assigning *Iphigeneia in Tauris,* though certain scenes have tragic overtones. Four plays I should call indisputably tragicomedies—*Alcestis, Helen, Ion,* and *Orestes.* I should be inclined, though with slightly less conviction, to add the satyr play, the *Cyclops.* All of these fit the requirements of tragicomedy as I have defined them. And lest it appear that my set of three is simply a description of these five plays, let me add that this definition of tragicomedy may be meaningfully applied, in my opinion, to a host of literary works outside the Greek tradition.

The *Cyclops* clearly offers a discrepancy between content and treatment. Cannibalism in itself strikes me as tragicomic subject matter par excellence. The idea of having the hero end up as a pot roast, or even threatened with such a fate, is simply too grotesque for tragedy. It so overemphasizes the purely animal side of man that—at least artistically—the attitude of human revolt cannot be sustained. At the same time, while we can laugh at cannibalism in the abstract—witness *New Yorker* cartoons—we can hardly accept it as funny when it involves someone we have come to know, even if he is but a stage character. The *Cyclops* exploits this ambivalence. Odysseus reacts to the eating of his companions with appropriate horror. Silenus and the satyrs regard it all as unfortunate but quite to be expected, and they carry on with the usual buffoonery. Similarly Silenus' betrayal, the satyrs' cowardice, and the pain of the blinded Cyclops are treated comically. Yet treachery, pain, and blindness are not ordinarily regarded as funny. Content and dramatic style are at variance. If we look for deeper meaning and interpret the play as the encounter of civilization and barbarism, the ambiguity is intensified. The civilized hero wins out, but only after having displayed a barbarity scarcely surpassed by that of his host, beginning with theft, proceeding with torture, concluding with a boastful exultation over his enemy that can be read only as hubris and which is followed by the prophecy of Nemesis to come. Such basic ironies in the story itself and the disparity between theme and treatment make the *Cyclops* a tragicomedy, not merely a peculiar hybrid or parody in which the conventional form of tragedy is burlesqued. The mood of the *Cyclops* is comparable to Voltaire's *Candide,* which elicits the same combination of horror and amusement, pity and disgust, and which is certainly a tragicomic novel if there ever was one.

The other four dramas are admittedly different in that they are more serious, contain none of the downright ribaldry of the *Cyclops,* and present more carefully drawn characters. *Alcestis* and *Helen,* despite the obvious differences in their plots and themes, are similar in their way of rejecting both the tragic and the comic points of view. In each drama the playwright has chosen to work with a genuine problem, for which he provides a solution which virtually denies its seriousness; that is, he wipes out the fundamental discrepancy. The dramas are alike, too, in that they are a blend of realism and fantasy, shifting in tone from heroic to comic.

In *Alcestis,* which we know was fourth in a tetralogy, the drunken Heracles has been regarded as a kind of substitute satyr, amusingly out of place in the tragic context. But the scene in its very inappropriateness has an edge to it, an underlying horror. It is tragicomic rather than comic. Earlier episodes are only slightly less so. Pheres' and Admetus' exchange of insults, as each taunts the other with his reluctance to die, is a bitingly satirical portrayal of these two unheroic heroes. Nor do I believe that Euripides was unaware of the ridiculous quality of Admetus' declaration that he will have a statue made of Alcestis and treat it as his wife. Or his invitation to her to come visit him in his dreams. Or his boasts that not even the powers of Hades could have prevented him from bringing Alcestis back from death—if only he had been lucky enough to have the gifts of Orpheus. All of this to the wife who is dying for him, whom he could save by the simple act of refusing her sacrifice!

This ironic treatment is perfectly suited to an intrinsically tragicomic plot. Alcestis herself is certainly a tragic heroine, and the play explores issues appropriate to tragedy—the conflict between the love that makes one willing to die for another and the human reluctance to leave life and the other; the question of whether anyone is ever justified in accepting such a sacrifice; even the problem of whether any one sex or class or type is intrinsically more valuable than another. But the solution is accomplished by a sort of magic which cancels out all tragic dilemma. In real life, the proof of ultimate devotion is not rewarded by an outsider coming in to wrestle with Death on one's behalf. Nor is a second chance given to a husband, whom only the death of his wife can awaken to an understanding of both her and himself.

Euripides' *Helen* plays with this same sort of fairy-tale wish-fulfillment. The escape from Egypt is a necessary dramatic device if there is to be any action at all. The real theme is Helen's and Menelaus' rediscovery of each other. Following the legend that only a cloud-image of Helen went to Troy, Euripides combines realistic psychological reactions with pure fantasy. If read allegorically, the story might be interpreted as Menelaus' gradual acceptance—under persuasive feminine influence—of the image of the Helen he remembered at Sparta, to replace that of the faithless one at Troy for whom he had been fighting. The suggestion that some such allegorical meaning is present lends a certain gravity to the drama. Euripides, however, does not press it. Instead he exploits the incredulous joy of the desolate and disillusioned pair confronting a miracle which common sense declares impossible. Euripides subtly implies that Helen has been just a little impatient at having preserved her virtue, alone, without maintaining her reputation. There is both comedy and pathos in Menelaus' efforts to believe, against all reason, that his wife had not betrayed him after all. Tragicomedy is still keener when he prepares to kill Helen if their plan fails, not quite daring (and why should he?) to trust her promise to slay herself rather than submit to another lover. The drama presents miraculous deliverance after total tragedy; conflicts are not erased but declared never to have existed.

Alcestis and *Helen* have many literary parallels. Eliot's *The Cocktail Party,* remotely derived from *Alcestis,* is a tragicomedy which again closes up the discrepancies unrealistically. So does Graham Greene's *The Potting Shed,* with its literal resurrection from the dead. And I should include here those works which, like Huxley's *Time Must Have a Stop* and Hesse's *Siddhartha,* are based on monistic theories of reincarnation which simultaneously recognize the experience of human suffering and deny its ultimate reality.

Ion illustrates a third kind of tragicomic possibilities, that which stems from a discrepancy between the attitude of the protagonists and that of the spectators. Critics have pointed out that the romantic plot anticipates New Comedy. In bare outline it does. But the problem of what judgment we are to pass on the behavior of Apollo is essential, and it differentiates the play sharply not only from New Comedy, but from *Iphigeneia in Tauris.* The happiness of the ending is underscored by all concerned. Athena, Ion, Creusa, all keep assuring themselves and us that all has turned out well and that Apollo must be given credit for having benevolently planned everything from the beginning. (The rape, too, one wonders?) But the spectator cannot readily swallow all this. He cannot help remembering Ion's shock that the god could be an ordinary seducer, or Creusa's earlier statement that even if Apollo should finally straighten matters out, he could not erase the long years of sorrow.

Furthermore, we have been made to feel too much sympathy for
Xuthus for us to be willing to have him kept in the dark about
who his supposed son really is. When all is said and done, Apollo
has arranged to make Xuthus a kind of unwitting cuckold. Presumably this family will live happily ever after, like the prince and
the princess in the fairy tale, but the audience goes home with its
suspicions about this world confirmed.

Orestes is a tragicomedy which displays all three of the traits
which I have listed. The scene between Orestes and the Phrygian
slave illustrates the discrepancy between actual content and treatment. Orestes' resolve to kill the slave, quite needlessly, is brutal and
horrifying. His decision to let the Phrygian live seems almost to
result from amusement at watching him beg for his life, a kind of
thank-you for entertainment and flattery. Watching it, we experience
the same mingling of revulsion at what is happening and pleasurable
appreciation of the humorous way in which it is done. Other scenes
present a similarly ironic mixture. The conclusion of the play is no
genuine solution. Apollo resolves the conflict by divine fiat, but
there is no suggestion that his words correspond to any inward
change in the protagonists (as happens in Sophocles' *Philoctetes,* for
example) or that he represents a principle of abstract justice (as in
the *Oresteia*). One cannot possibly imagine that this heavenly vision
will leave Hermione happy to live with the man who wanted to
murder her, or that Orestes and Menelaus will be mutually respect-
ing father- and son-in-law, or that Orestes and the Argives will
happily cooperate in their government. Even more than in the *Ion,*
the fictional beings are satisfied, but we who are onlookers feel that
we have encountered only depravity where we expected heroism,
that if there is any rational justice here at all, it lies in the fact that
these villains deserve one another. Yet there remains just the slight-
est trace of pity for them in that they, too, are victims of others' evil
acts which gave rise to their present situations.

With *Orestes,* as with the rest of this group of Euripides' plays,
we are left with ambivalent feelings, aware that we cannot quite
sum it all up, either intellectually or emotionally, in any clear statement or attitude. This seems to me the very essence of tragicomedy.
All drama poses a question. Tragedy and comedy, each in its own
way, give distinctive answers. Tragicomedy indicates that when all
has been said on all sides, the question remains, and one still does
not quite know whether or not to take it seriously.

"Conversion" in Euripides

by William Arrowsmith

Nobody, I suppose, outside of classical studies, any longer reads either of A. W. Verrall's delightfully systematic distortions of Euripides, those two engaging and outrageous books, *Four Plays of Euripides* and *Euripides the Rationalist*. Yet Verrall as a critic bears rereading, less for his rationalist hypothesis, which hopelessly trapped his perceptions, than for the acuteness of those perceptions and his lucid and suggestive wrongheadedness. Indeed, I sometimes suspect that the reason classicists, apart from their native dislike of novelty, have been slow to adopt the techniques of the New Criticism is that Verrall (along with Samuel Butler) parodied and abused them before they formally existed, and so put the classicists off for half a century.

I have myself no wish to put anyone off, not even to put the New Critics off with Verrall. My use here for Verrall is mainly cautionary: I once had the unhappy but common experience of out-Verralling Verrall on *The Cocktail Party,* and I have no wish to repeat that performance, even if I could muster the necessary ingenuity. But I also wish to discuss Euripides' dramatic structure in relation to Eliot's comedy in the hope of making the much greater dramatist illustrate the methods and also (what I take to be) the failure of the lesser. For, unless I am badly mistaken, Eliot's Christian New Comedy of conversion is structurally very close to the movement, though not the meaning, of Euripidean drama. And Verrall, on the crucial point, comes pat to the comparison.

Verrall's theory of Euripidean structure will be immediately intelligible to anyone who has read even a little of recent Melville criticism. It rests entirely on two perceptions, both of which seem

" 'Conversion' in Euripides" (editor's title) by William Arrowsmith. From "The Comedy of T. S. Eliot," in English Stage Comedy, ed. W. K. Wimsatt, Jr. (New York: Columbia University Press, 1955), pp. 148-56. Copyright 1955 by Columbia University Press. Reprinted by permission of the publisher.

to me indisputably accurate. First is what might be called Euripides'
quarrel with the gods of Olympos, that transparent rationalism in
the tradition of Xenophanes that makes him surround such myths
as Leda's egg or Thyestes' feast with a dubious "so men say" or "the
story goes"; or, even more strongly, his outright assertion that the
logoi of the Homeric gods are "the wretched tales of poets." Second,
Verrall noticed that in play after play there comes a point where the
literal action as dramatized cannot be accepted without gross inconsistency or intolerable paradox; the play appears to say one
thing and to dramatize it as real, and then to assert somehow an
antithetical reality. Thus in the *Herakles,* for instance, the hero is
shown suffering madness as the result of the direct intervention of
the goddess Hera's agents, Iris and Madness herself; yet later in
same play Herakles boldly asserts a principle whose apparent consequence is the denial of the reality of the experience out of which
the assertion is made in the first place. Herakles, that is, simply
denies that the actions of the gods could in fact be such as they have
been dramatized to be.

On the basis of these two perceptions, and this suggestion of a
double pattern of reality in the plays, Verrall inferred that two
simultaneous actions were being presented on two simultaneous
"levels": the superficial action was "ostensible" and the profounder
action was "real." By an ostensible plot Verrall meant one so con-
structed as to give no offense to the vulgar and pious when dealing
with received religious traditions, an action which presented "things
as they are said to be," *as if* they were real, while the real action
was a human story entirely divested of the improbable or fabulous.
In order to provide this double plot with a double audience, Verrall assumed an elite of *sophoi,* rationalist intellectuals who would
see through the ostensible absurdities and enjoy the real play in
all its rationalist rigor. The theory was then reapplied to the plays
with almost pathological ingenuity, and with atrocious results.
Thus Alkestis never really died (for Euripides was too sensible to
believe in the nonsense of regeneration), while the great labors of
Herakles and his harrowing of Hades were all fictive disguises for
the real tragedy of a great man who struggled, not under the lash
of a god-driven necessity, but merely with his own megalomania.
And so on, with hideous rigor of application, throughout most of
the Euripidean corpus.

Yet for all the visible absurdity of Verrall's conclusions, his theory
should command more respect than it does. At least it seems to
me both more perceptive and more courageous than most Euripi-

dean criticism with its outraged Aristotelian literalness and its perpetual cry of formal botching and inconsistency. Verrall's own mistake came, I think, not in his double-reality pattern, but in the hypothesis which was meant to mirror what he saw, that division of the play into two continuous levels of action, real and apparent, each autonomous and complete. The worst that can be said of Verrall's theory is that its elaboration was first unnecessary and then untruthful; and in this it appears to me to resemble most critical theories which operate everywhere on the assumption of parallel levels of reality, or of real and apparent meanings. We need, I think, a greater sense of the variety of ways in which reality gets into literature, and I personally wish it were more often possible in contemporary criticism to preserve, for appropriate writers, the notion of reality as apparently fortuitous, and even casual, to keep respect for the simple, formal rightness of luck in things that happen. Verrall certainly had no such respect, and his criticism must pay the cost of a reality so terribly schematized as to be that much less a reality.

It should be obvious by now in what sense Verrall's theory of Euripidean structure is cautionary for Eliot. And perhaps it is too obvious, but in almost all the criticism of Eliot's two comedies with which I am familiar, the crucial difficulty has come in stating precisely just what relationship obtains between the secular framework of the plot and the constant hints of another, and Christian, reality. Are we meant to take the physical cocktail party as the empty vehicle of Christian communion? Do we have two continuous Verrallian "levels," one secular and one Christian? Or is the connection between the doublet reality of the play merely adventitious and momentary, a sudden irruption of the Christian real into the secular terms of the play, illuminating and transfiguring them?

Both Euripides and Eliot present in their plays a double reality, and a Euripidean play no more consists of an "ostensible" action superimposed on a "real" one than an Eliot play consists of one Christian and one secular action. The relation between the two realities is variously systematic and adventitious, and the term I suggest for their connection is that of "conversion"—if, for a moment, I can use the word without its religious connotations. By "conversion" I mean simply the transfiguration of one action or its terms, a conversion or transformation of one reality to another —but not an "epiphany" and not a conversion of "levels."

The commonest form of such conversion in Euripides is that in which a story (i.e., a *logos*) derived from received beliefs—the world

of myth and the corpus of "things as they are said to be"—is suddenly, in all of its parts—its terms, its characters, and the values it
invokes—"converted," under dramatic pressure, to another phase
of reality. What we get is something like a dramatic mutation of
conventional or traditional reality, and the leap the play makes
between the phases or plateaus of its two realities is meant to
correspond, in force and vividness and apparent unpredictability,
to mutations in the physical world. It is this violence in the conversion of reality that explains the wrenching dislocation of Euripidean drama from an Aristotelian point of view, and the apparent
lack of necessary connection between the parts of the play. The
play pivots on two seemingly incompatible realities, and if it insists on the greater reality of what has been dramatically created
over what has been traditionally received, it does not do so by
denying validity to received reality, but subtly displaces it in the
transfiguration of its terms. Euripidean structure mirrors in this
way both the artist's intent and his possibilities. Because Euripides
is dramatizing the incongruities of a culture—its received values
against its actual or ideal values—he must at least allow dignity
of reality to the values which the play supersedes. And at least one
consequence of such a method is clearly psychological strain for
his characters, who have to bear the intolerable burden of the cultural disparity which the play dramatizes. Thus in the *Orestes,* for
instance, the matricide is presented in a world in which the institution of civil justice already exists, and, in consequence, Orestes'
action exposes his own criminal nature, rather than being, as in
the *Oresteia,* a god-driven deed which leads to the creation of civil
justice.

   In no play is this conversion of reality more sharp than in the
Herakles. Here two savagely different actions, one conventional and
the other set in a world where tradition is dumb and conduct un-
charted, are jammed harshly against each other, and the collision
of their values is stressed by the most violent peripety of Greek
tragedy. The first action is static and conventional melodrama,
wholly informed by "things as they are said to be," and rounded
off with a cozy and traditionalized theodicy in which hybris is
punished and virtue rewarded by the benevolent and vindicated
gods. Herakles himself is presented essentially as Pindar had left
him: the great culture-hero of enormous physical strength, self-
sufficient and bearing on his back all the values of aristocratic *aretē.*
His civilizing labors and his harrowing of Hades are accepted as

literal truths, and the ambiguity in tradition which made Herakles the son of two fathers, Zeus and Amphitryon, is sustained.

Against such a background, the second action breaks with tragic force and striking transformations, showing first the conquering hero, the *kallinikos,* reduced to tears, helpless, dependent, and in love, stripped of that outward strength which until now had exempted him from normal human necessity, and discovering both his common ground with men and the internalized courage of the human hero confronting his condition. And point for point, each of the terms that was appropriate to the Herakles of tradition is transformed and displaced. Thus Amphitryon becomes Herakles' "real" father, not by the fact of conception, but by the fact of love, *philia,* while the literal descent to Hades is transformed in the refusal to die and the courage which, under an intolerable necessity, perseveres. The old Hades of the poets, with its Sisyphos, Cerberos, and torments, is transformed into the Hades within, here and now, as Herakles himself declares: "And I am like Ixion, chained forever to a flying wheel." So too the old labors are replaced by the metaphorical sense of the labors of human life and the cost of civilization, while the goddess Hera, who in myth made Herakles mad and the destroyer of his sons, demonstrates her own incredibility as a goddess and passes almost insensibly into a hovering symbol of all those irrational and random necessities which the Greeks and the play call *Tukhe,* and which we limply translate as "Fortune."

All these conversions replace and dislodge, but do not disown, the first action by transfiguring it at every point. The first action is neither false nor even unreal, but it is inadequate. Through the force of contrast with its own transfiguration it comes to seem obsolete, naive, or even humdrum, much as fresh conviction, formed under *peine forte et dure,* insensibly makes the conviction it replaces naive or jejune in comparison. Under the changed light of experience and the pattern it imposes, what was once taken for reality comes to seem illusion at best: true while held as true, but with widened experience discovered inadequate. And what we see is less the contradiction between the two opposed realities than the counterpointed relation of their development, the way in which, under the blow of experience and insight, one reality is made to yield a further one, each geared to its appropriate experience. We begin with a familiar and conventional world, operating from familiar motives in a field of accepted, though outmoded, values; by the time the play closes, character, motives, and values

have all been transfigured and pushed to the very frontiers of
reality.

What Verrall saw with great clarity was the defeat of one reality
by another in Euripides, and he correctly observed that the victorious reality was essentially a rationalized one. But because he assumed the connection between them was precisely that between
false illusion and natural reality, rather than a series of discrete
conversions, he stultified the plays and distorted their direction.
He observed, that is, the rationalization of the fabulous and the
outmoded or barbarous supernatural in Euripides; but he failed
to notice that this rationalization was not final, that Euripides more
often than not discredits the fabulous only in order to make it good,
to re-earn it, on a symbolic or a metaphorical level. Illusion is not
merely exposed, but it is first exposed and then transfigured or
"converted." Thus Verrall rightly assumed that Euripides believed
neither in Hades nor in the physical regeneration of Alkestis, but
ignored the moral and metaphorical equivalent of her "death."
For the point of the *Alkestis* is surely not, as Verrall thought, that
Alkestis neither really died nor went to Hades, but that she had
to "die" if Admetos, and hence herself, were ever to be "reborn."
But as Eliot saw and put it in *The Cocktail Party,* the crux of the
Alkestis is, after all, that moral death is the condition of moral rebirth; that Admetos (like Edward) must, even at the risk of apparent weakness, take back his wife from Herakles' hands as a new
woman or not at all. But, obsessed by his own rationalist convic-
tions and encouraged by Euripides' clear commitment to *this*
world, Verrall imposed upon the plays a crude rationalism foreign
to them, and he distorted their structure accordingly.

Between Euripides and Verrall, then, there is some small common ground in an initial rationalism; and while structurally
Euripides does possess a doublet-reality, his plays are actually not
doublet on two levels but complex conversions.

The Ironic Structure in *Alcestis*

by Wesley D. Smith

There are two distinguishable structures in *Alcestis*, the combination of which makes the drama. The primary structure is the melodramatic plot: Admetus is saved from misfortune because he entertains Heracles who in turn rescues Alcestis—the plot predicted by Apollo in the prologue (64-72). It is melodramatic because of the kind of events involved and because of the tone in which it is related. Death is the villain of the piece, and Heracles is the hero who rescues the noble husband's virtuous wife at the last possible moment. The other is an ironic structure, parallel to the first, composed of themes, imagery, and even a kind of plot—the testing of Admetus. The melodramatic plot offers an exposition and interpretation of the Alcestis myth. Concurrently the ironic plot offers an analysis and criticism of the attitudes and beliefs implied by the melodramatic plot and by the myth itself.

This is not to say that the poet offers two plays in *Alcestis*, one for the ordinary spectator and another for the discerning, but rather that both treatments of the story, which imply different readings of the same facts, are necessarily available to all of the audience, and that fully to appreciate the play requires responding to both. Critics have recognized a compounding of styles in the play. It has been treated as a comedy which also offers a serious, perhaps tragic character study in Admetus, and the label tragi-comedy is frequently applied. But as in many of Euripides' experiments in mixing tones and styles within a single play, the combination is unique, and therefore difficult to classify usefully. I shall use the terms melodramatic, tragic, and comic to describe particular effects used by Euripides, without defining a class to which the play belongs.

"The Ironic Structure in Alcestis*" by Wesley D. Smith. From* The Phoenix, *XIV (1960), 127-45. Copyright 1960 by The Classical Association of Canada and the University of Toronto Press. Reprinted by permission of the author and publishers. Some notes have been omitted or abbreviated, and English translations have been supplied by Professor Smith.*

This study of *Alcestis* attempts to demonstrate that the treatment
of Admetus' character and the variety of effects employed are elements in a single design intended as a critical analysis of the myth's
implications.

In the prologue Euripides emphasizes melodramatic elements already present in the myth.[1] For noble and pious Admetus there are
great difficulties, but great possibilities. The dark inexorable forces
represented by Thanatos can be conquered, and, as the audience
learns, will be by a timely intervention. Thus prepared, the audience can follow Euripides' development of what the myth implies
as an interpretation of human and divine relationships, and as an
evaluation of nobility, marriage, and death and resurrection. But the
melodramatic fairy-tale of death and resurrection is unrealistic, not
in the technical sense in which all dramatic presentation that depends on convention is unrealistic, but in the sense that the events
which are conventionally represented do not seem to refer to reality
or to be subject to its limitations. And values and behaviour dependent on such constructions are also unrealistic. When explored
they appear to be a burlesque of what the real world requires. Something like that is what Euripides demonstrates through the dual
form of his play. At the same time as he elaborates the philosophy
inherent in the myth, he also burlesques it, satirizes it, or treats it
ironically through his thematic structure, and suggests alternatives.

The term "irony," hackneyed as it may be, appears to me to be
the most useful and accurate term for describing Euripides' method,
in *Alcestis* and elsewhere, of presenting a point of view and at the
same time qualifying or contradicting it by means of a satirical
treatment.[2] The technique is obviously related to what we normally

[1] The exact shape of the myth before Euripides is uncertain. Wilamowitz
conjectured that it was part of the Coronis story in the Hesiodic *Eoiae*, but
evidence is slight (*Philologische Untersuchungen* 9 [1885] especially pp. 65-73).
Attempts to reconstruct Phrynichus' play also fail from lack of evidence, e.g.,
H. L. Ebeling, *TAPA* 29 (1898) 65-85. More dependable is the approach of Albin
Lesky, who demonstrates the myth's dependence on folk-tale themes, characters,
and events (*Akad. der Wiss. in Wien*, Sb. B.203, Ab. 2 [1925] 57-76). A. M. Dale,
in her commentary on *Alcestis*, offers a judicious review of available evidence
(Oxford 1954) vii-xvii.

[2] "Irony is the most general term that we have for the kind of qualification
which the various elements in a context receive from the context" (Cleanth
Brooks, *The Well Wrought Urn* [New York 1947] 209). Compare J. A. K. Thom-
son on Euripides' "modern" use of dramatic irony, *Irony* (London 1926) 70-92.
R. P. Winnington-Ingram uses the term "satire" to describe Euripides' treatment
of the god Dionysus, and says: "The satire is of a piece with the other work of
Euripides; it was a part of his mind" (*Euripides and Dionysus* [Cambridge
1948] 27). The term is too limited, however, for my purposes.

think of as dramatic irony, i.e., dramatic use of a contrast between appearance and reality in speech or action based on what the audience knows is an incomplete understanding of the situation ("Whoever killed Laius—who knows?—might want to take vengeance on me, too."), and is related also to Socratic irony, i.e., understatement which offers an apparently false surface meaning but which points to a profounder truth beneath ("I know nothing."), but it is not the same as either. For comparison, an example of Euripides' characteristic irony from *Alcestis* will be useful: Death is presented in the prologue and final scene as a bullying coward, a democrat, and a bad wrestler. Foolish on the surface, and incompatible with normal feelings about death, still this proves to be an accurate picture of the character Death as required by the myth of Alcestis' resurrection. But the emphatic overdrawing of that character, normally referred to as one of the comic elements in the play, constitutes a satire on the character while it is being drawn, and so offers satirical perspective on the myth, and suggests that a truer picture of life and death than that offered by the myth is available. The treatment of Death is exemplary of what Euripides does throughout the play, and, with apologies for the broadness of the term, I shall call it irony. For purposes of analysis I shall distinguish various uses of this irony—in characterization, in elaboration of themes, and in manipulation of the plot. They are not to be conceived separately, but as elements in the single ironic structure Euripides offers as a treatment of the Alcestis myth.⁷

Characterization of Admetus

Admetus is characterized from two points of view: as the worthy friend of god and demigod, whose character inspires others to help him, and as a self-centred, cowardly, and short-sighted man. The views need not be contradictory. The second view, though thoroughly developed, is developed almost totally by indirection, by irony, except in the scene with Pheres. In Admetus' own estimation, and in that of Apollo, Heracles, and the chorus, and presumably in the myth as received, Admetus is a noble and decent man who is treated badly by fate, and who loses his generous wife as a result. He is treated by all the characters except his father as a king who deserves respect. He describes himself as a man of honour and of noble passions, concerned for his reputation. But even before his first entrance an insistent ironic tone is introduced in references to

him, which chips away at that estimable character and gives the
impression that there is something else underneath.⌉

After the initial sympathetic and complimentary references to
Admetus by Apollo and the chorus (10 ff., 78 ff.), very little is said
by or about Admetus that does not invite the audience to form its
own estimate of him, different from his own. The exchange at 144-
145, which is often cited as a statement damaging to Admetus, might
pass without the audience's finding any ambiguity, but there follows
to reinforce it:

Chorus. Is not something useful being done for Alcestis?
Servant. Yes, the clothes are ready with which her husband will bury her.
(148-149)[3]

After the maidservant's moving description of Alcestis' preparations
for, and emotions about death, the chorus wants to know what
Admetus is feeling:

Chorus.   I suppose Admetus is grieving in such troubles, since he has to be
            deprived of a good wife?
Servant. He is weeping and holding his wife in his hands and begging her
            not to betray him, seeking the impossible. (199-203)

The picture is vivid, and "seeking the impossible" has often been
noticed, but there is a subtler effect involved also. The word "betray" is out of place. Its significance, and the force of its repetitions
are often obscured, but Euripides uses the word προδοῦναι, though
weaker words were available, for a purpose. Shortly before, the
maidservant has reported Alcestis' words to her bed: "I do not
hate you, though you have destroyed me only, for I die because I
am unwilling to *betray* you and my husband" (179-181). Admetus'
echo of these words is unfortunate. It gives exactly the wrong tone

---

[3] Euripides is punning on the words πρόσφορα [useful objects], προσφορά [gifts
for the dead], and ἐκφορά [carrying out to burial], a pun which he will use again,
adding δύσφορα [things difficult to bear] (617, 739). Aristophanes appreciated the
pun, apparently, and recalled it when he parodied *Alcestis* 367-368: "Carry her
out, for not even in death may I ever be separated from you, O pickled-in-beets."
Dicaearchus means "Carry her out and cook her (the eel)." In his reception of
the eel Dicaearchus parodies, in reverse order, Admetus' farewell to his wife
(*Acharnians* 893-894—*Alcestis* 367-368) and his later recognition of her (*Ach.*
885—*Alc.* 1133, *Ach.* 891—*Alc.* 1132). How Aristophanes staged the parody
(using veil, bier, etc.) one can only guess, but I am convinced that the success of
the parody depends on the audience's previous recognition of the humorous
irony that is in *Alcestis*, and therefore that it is evidence for contemporary
understanding of the play's ironies.

to what he says. But this report of his words might pass the audience
by if he did not repeat the words twice on stage during Alcestis'
death scene (250, 275). The idea of betrayal, so introduced and
emphasized, is used for a purpose beyond that of immediate characterizing irony. The idea of betrayal, and the question of what is
betrayal are made into a theme in the play, and finally are the
subject of the final scene.[4]

The promise made by the ironies preceding Admetus' entrance is
fulfilled when he appears. Admetus' first words on stage, in answer
to Alcestis' address to the heavens, are: "They see you and me, two
sufferers who have done nothing to the gods for which you should
die" (246-247). His words remind the audience of Apollo's part in
her death, as well as of Admetus' own part.[5] The attitude that
Admetus exhibits in his first speech is the one that he maintains
throughout. What he finds most notable in his wife's death is his
own suffering, and there is a certain exorbitance in all that he says,
and an incongruity: "This speech I hear of yours is sadder than all
of death for me." "With you dead I could not live." "In you do we
exist, to live or not" (273-274, 278, 279). One cannot help being reminded, by all that Admetus says, of the "true" situation: Alcestis'
death is a bargain to keep Admetus alive. That what he says is
spoken as though on another occasion only reminds the audience
more insistently. It is not Admetus' sincerity that is brought into
question by such ironies or by the long list of things he and his
subjects will give up for his dead wife (who asks only one thing).
His emotions are genuine enough, but one is led to look more
closely at the man who has such emotions at such a time.

The chorus is almost unwavering in its sympathy and admiration
for Admetus. They have some suspicion that bad taste is involved
in forcing entertainment on Heracles immediately after the death.
But they are quickly convinced (551-567).[6] The same is true of
Heracles, who thinks highly of Admetus throughout except for his
brief suspicion that Admetus has insulted him by lying to him
(808 ff.). But if one listens to the words of the play the irony is

---

[4] For the development of the betrayal theme see lines 202, 250, 275, 290, 659,
1058, 1096. For connection with dishonour note 658, and *cf.* 567, 373, and the
final scene, to be discussed below.

[5] Note the similar effect from the use of παιᾶνα in 424. One does not normally
sing a paean while carrying out one's wife's corpse.

[6] Note, however, the touch of satire at the end of Admetus' convincing explanation. He gives one too many reasons, and his "Argos is a thirsty place"
calls up visions of future symposia that he does not intend to miss (560, *cf.* 343-
344).

always there. For example it is possible, though not entirely normal, for a man to say on the occasion of his wife's death: "I should never have married and lived with her in this house. I envy the unmarried and those who have no children. There is one life, and grief for it is a reasonable burden" (880-884, *cf.* 238 ff. and note the reversal of 712). But such a statement is not possible for Admetus whose wife has given him her life also in behalf of her children. The chorus consoles Admetus by saying: "A man with a grief like yours could cut his throat or hang himself" (228-230), and later with: "There was a man in my family whose poor son died in his house—an only child. But he bore up well enough, though childless, though he was getting gray, and was well along in life" (903 ff.). Both are good and recognizable sentiments for consolation, but hardly appropriate for Admetus. The second recalls for the audience the earlier scene in which Admetus, an only child, berated his father for being willing to survive him, and suggested that Pheres would be better off dead than bereft of Admetus. Yet the chorus cites a man in exactly Pheres' situation who bore up well enough. Scholars, perplexed by the anomaly, have explained away the force of the reference by conjecturing that Euripides is here taking the opportunity to refer to Anaxagoras or another contemporary known to himself and the audience. But since it is Admetus' family that is in question in *Alcestis* the audience should understand the reference readily enough as another ironic comment on the stage action and emotion of the moment.

It would be tedious to pursue the ironies through every statement. What is important is that the play is organized in such a way as to offer continual opportunity for such treatment of its story. The effect of the ironies is to prod the audience toward a critical view. Though Admetus' emotions are dramatized throughout, the audience is never allowed to relax into sympathy with him. Even the numerous formulae of consolation and mourning do not suffice to set the play's tone, since wit intrudes and the formulae are put to ironic use.[7] One can deny that Admetus deserves criticism, and produce reasons of state, family, or *Zeitgeist* which justify Admetus in behaving as he did, and so prevent the audience from concluding that Admetus might have done otherwise than to accept the sacrifice of Alcestis. But instead Euripides

---

[7] There is another reason also why the great amount of mourning does not set the play's tone. Another kind of irony is operating as well—the dramatic irony that comes from the audience's expectation that Alcestis will be restored. The audience is not invited to share in the grief.

has contented himself with making such reasons conspicuously absent, and with characterizing Admetus in such a way as to suggest the later career of the kind of man who would solicit and accept such a sacrifice. Whoever is carried away with Admetus finds himself brought up short eventually, by a statue in his bed ("a frigid delight," 353), by inappropriately phrased sympathy from the chorus, or by a piece of verbal wit aimed at the hero's idea of himself.

The Pheres scene, the central scene of the play, offers a frontal attack on Admetus, both in the things Pheres says and in the unpleasant similarities between father and son that are revealed. By the end of the scene the audience has little use for the man who exits to the funeral with an unconscious pun about his wife's corpse.[8] The characterization is complete. But between the funeral and the final scene Admetus returns to the stage to repeat his grief, and to suggest that he is a changed man. And finally he is partially convincing, despite the continuing ironies, not because of his insistence that life means nothing to him (866-871, 895-902, 935-940), which we have heard before (276-278, 347, 382, 386), but because he foresees now specific and real problems which arise from his vows to Alcestis, and he seems to be preparing to face them (944-953). He also faces more directly what he had heard from Pheres, but did not comprehend before (954-961; *cf.* 694-705). He does not consider the possibility that Pheres may be right, but he feels that his reputation is gone, and that his enemies will say he is a coward. Therefore life is unbearable.

While Admetus laments this situation, and seems to grow in awareness, the audience waits for him to draw a significant conclusion, such as "I should never have allowed her to die in my place." But the poet is only tantalizing the audience. Admetus will say anything but that. The poet brings him to the brink of such a statement in the famous ἄρτι μανθάνω [now I realize] speech. But at most Admetus can conclude—and this is the substance of his

---

8

> ἡμεῖς δέ, τοὺν ποσὶν γὰρ οἰστέον κακόν,
> στείχωμεν, ὡς ἄν ἐν πυρᾷ θῶμεν νεκρόν.   739-740

[As for us, since we must bear the evils which are at our feet, let us go now and put the corpse on the pyre.]

(*cf.* footnote 3). A. W. Verrall, *Euripides the Rationalist* (Cambridge 1895), 127, comments on the emphatic position of this couplet, to which the rhyme would perhaps contribute.

realization—that Alcestis is better off than he (935 ff.). It seems ungracious of him to say so, and so to rob her sacrifice of value. She, at least, believed that there was nothing more precious than her gift to him. Nevertheless the scene does offer a suggestion of growth and change in Admetus, and keeps his character interesting into the last scene where a final use is made of the double characterization (*infra*, "The Testing of Admetus").

Euripides never suggests specifically what Admetus should have done, either in the beginning when he was soliciting the sacrifice or later when he had received it. Instead the ironic characterization is strictly negative—a running commentary which hints at kinds of motivation and qualities of character beneath the surface. By preventing the audience from accepting Admetus at his own valuation, Euripides requires that they maintain a certain distance, and reconsider from their own point of view the human problems and values inherent in the myth. The terms for the audience's reconsideration are suggested by recurrent themes and by words Admetus has always in his mouth: loyalty, nobility, betrayal, baseness.]

Themes

Through recurrent themes the Greek dramatist makes clear his reason for being attracted to the traditional material he has chosen for his play, and for shaping it in the way that he has. Justice in the *Oresteia*, sight and knowledge in *Oedipus Tyrannus*, friendship and chance in *Heracles* are examples of themes which point in the direction of the dramatist's purpose in those plays, and through which one must seek the meaning the poet draws from the myth he has chosen.[Euripides has made three themes particularly prominent in *Alcestis*: good breeding, death and its meaning, and the house and family. All three are used as elements both in the melodramatic structure and in the ironic structure.]

As the chorus says in the third stasimon, commenting on Admetus' action in bringing Heracles into the house under false pretenses: "Good breeding makes a man virtuous, and leads him instinctively, in spite of himself, to do the right thing" (600 ff.). [The chorus has proof of its conclusions: Admetus treated Apollo well and acted as the perfect host even when he need not have, and as a result he was rewarded with prosperity and continued life by Apollo (570 ff., *cf*. 6-14). Perhaps, hopes the chorus, his entertainment of Heracles will have similarly good results. The chorus was shocked at first

(551 ff.), but cannot imagine that Admetus' good breeding would play him false. Surely good will come from the apparent breach of manners. Of course the chorus is correct.

Heracles, too, is conscious of the obligations of a gentleman, and when he discovers that Admetus has lied to him he is not such a boor as to interpet Admetus' behaviour unfairly, but echoing the chorus' sentiments he says:]

> He concealed his trouble, since he is well bred, out of respect ($\alpha\iota\delta\epsilon\sigma\theta\epsilon\iota s$) for me. What Thessalian loves guests more, what Greek? He will never say that he did a good turn to a base man, nobleman that he is. (857-860)

Heracles, in his own mind, is put to it to prove that he too has manners, and is not low born ($\kappa\alpha\kappa\acute{o}s$). As a result he rescues Alcestis, and so can speak freely, or as a free man, as Admetus' social and moral equal, after having done so ($\grave{\epsilon}\lambda\epsilon\upsilon\theta\acute{\epsilon}\rho\omega s$, 1008).[9] In this way the ideal of good breeding serves as the motive force in the action of the melodramatic plot.] Its use in the ironic structure is more complicated.

[Concern for social status is general among the male characters, but is especially associated with Admetus. He assures Alcestis that he will not marry again, because there will not be a girl from a good enough family (332-333). His memories of their wedding are memories of the guests' congratulations on how well born both the bridal pair were: both eupatrids, both from the aristocracy (915 ff.). The battle between Admetus and Pheres, which is introduced by the choral ode on good breeding, hinges on the standards of a gentleman, to which each finds the other inferior.[10] Through the Admetus-Pheres scene and elsewhere the theme of good breeding is developed with a semi-technical vocabulary: $\alpha\iota\delta\acute{\omega}s$ [sense of honor] and its derivatives, and $\grave{\epsilon}\lambda\epsilon\acute{\upsilon}\theta\epsilon\rho os$, (which in tragedy is used also for $\grave{\epsilon}\lambda\epsilon\upsilon\theta\acute{\epsilon}\rho\iota os$, i.e., both *liber* and *liberalis*) are added to the usual terms which describe nobility: $\kappa\alpha\lambda\acute{o}s$, $\check{\alpha}\rho\iota\sigma\tau os$, $\gamma\epsilon\nu\nu\alpha\hat{\iota}os$, $\kappa\tau\lambda$.[11]

Admetus is a gentleman, and the audience is assured that his manners are perfect as they apply to strangers and guests. He is

---

[9] This will perhaps appear to overemphasize the simple word $\grave{\epsilon}\lambda\epsilon\upsilon\theta\acute{\epsilon}\rho\omega s$ and for no purpose. The reason that it is a strong word is that the play puts such emphasis on good breeding and connects it with the term $\grave{\epsilon}\lambda\epsilon\acute{\upsilon}\theta\epsilon\rho os$ (569, cf. 638-641, 675-676). To insist that it means simply "candidly" in Heracles' mouth (Dale, xxiii) ignores his stated purpose in rescuing Alcestis.

[10] Note especially Admetus' self-defeating attempt at irony (636 ff.) and Pheres' answer to it (675 ff.).

[11] For the development and use of these terms see esp. 109-111, 194, 624, 636 ff., 702, 750, 857 ff.

φιλόξενος [a lover of guests] (809, 830, 858). But during the play he renounces kinship with his parents, the natural φίλοι, first implicitly and then explicitly (636 ff., 734 ff.), and when he is asked whether the "dead woman" is a member of his family he answers that she is a foreigner who came to live with him when her father died. She was simply a homeless person, an ὀθνεῖος, not even a guest. ὀθνεῖος in tragedy is used only in this play. Euripides uses and emphasizes the prose word in order to draw attention to Admetus' strange assertions as to who is φίλος [dear *or* belonging] to him (532, 533, 646, 810). The act is ambiguous. Admetus later offers the defence that his sudden tergiversation was required by noble motives of hospitality. It is noteworthy, however, that his view of the host's office requires denying the status of guest to the woman who was more than life to him shortly before. The problem will recur in the final scene.

In his nobility Admetus is like his father in all respects, not least in calculating the value of a wife in terms of profit and loss. Admetus says to the dying Alcestis that he hopes he can get some profit from the children, since Alcestis herself is bringing him not profit but grief, a calculation repeated by Eumelus and by Pheres in slightly different ways (334-335, 412, 628). Indeed the family of Pheres keeps a strict balance sheet of obligations within the family, and both Admetus and Pheres use it as a text in their argument (658 ff., 685 ff.).

In this way the theme of good breeding, combined with the φίλος-ὀθνεῖος [dear or belonging *vs.* not-belonging] theme and the theme of profit and loss, is used ironically to draw a contrast between the values invoked by Admetus and his family and the qualities that they exhibit. The contrast is between external and internal, public and private. The chorus and Heracles appreciate the external nobility of Admetus, while the audience, through Admetus' mirror-image Pheres and through the ironic treatment of Admetus and his claims, is led to appreciate also the private character of the man, and to judge it in Admetus' own terms of nobility.

A related theme, that of house and family, emphasizes the same contrast between internal and external, public and private. Admetus is conscious of his house as an institution, as an aristocratic dynasty. But contrasted with his concern for the house as institution is the feeling of the rest of its inhabitants for the house as home, as a quality of life. When the child says "With your death, mother, the house is dead" (414-415), he speaks not of the royal line but of the home. There is no technical vocabulary developed for the con-

trast, δόμος, οἶκος, and δῶμα being used interchangeably. Rather the
contrast is built on a series of associations which reveal what the
house means to the people who live in it.

Alcestis dies for her home, as she makes clear in her death scene
as well as in what the maidservant reports of her. To the goddess
of the hearth she gives her farewell prayer, addressing her as mistress
and entrusting the children to her (162 ff.). After putting suppliant
boughs at the other altars she addresses her bed, the symbol of
her marriage and home, which she would not betray by taking
another husband (177 ff., 284 ff.). She bids goodbye to all the household individually, stretching out her hand to each. "And there was
none so low-born (κακός) that she did not address him and receive
his address in return" (193-195).[12] Not the personal relationship with
her husband or distinctions of breeding, but her relationship with
the home which includes her husband is what we are told moves
Alcestis, and is what she talks about. There is no indication in the
play that Alcestis is disappointed in her husband in her final moments. Alcestis is not cold. All we see and hear of her shows her
single-minded and passionate about the house and family of which
Admetus is the head. Admetus characteristically mistakes the intention of her request that he not marry again, and assures her
that he cannot find as noble or pretty a girl as she, and does not
want any more children, and therefore will find his vow easy to
keep (328 ff.). Alcestis perhaps has reason to be disappointed, but
the text gives no indication that Euripides intended her to show it.

Of the inhabitants of the house, the audience sees, besides Alcestis
and Admetus, the children and two slaves. Their testimony is
unanimous that Alcestis was the home, as the boy says. Both servants
are primarily concerned with Alcestis (unlike the chorus), showing
her a loyalty like that she has shown to the home. Both depreciate
Admetus (201 ff., 145, 770 ff.). The second servant recalls Alcestis'
farewell to the household which the first had reported, and foresees
the house as it is to be: Alcestis had been like a mother to all the
household, softening her husband's rages. The same term is used by
Alcestis, who predicts that after her death time will soften Admetus'
grief, and is later used by Heracles, who predicts that time will
soften also his resolve of celibacy (381, 771, 1085).

⎡The house is prominent from the first word of the play to the

---

[12] This phrase is echoed by Alcestis herself in 312, a line that should not be
deleted. Admetus remembers it when he sees the empty house (942), and it is
recalled again when he asks whether he can address the silent Alcestis in 1131
(note also 1005). It unites the theme of good breeding with that of the house.

final exit of Admetus and Alcestis into the house. The house is the
stage setting, of course, and Apollo's opening speech is an address
to the house. Death enters there before the servant girl and later
Alcestis and Admetus come out. Heracles is entertained in one part
of the house while preparations for the funeral are going on in
another. The complementary views of the house as home and as
institution are elaborated separately, the former through Alcestis
herself and the household's memories of her, the latter through
Admetus' defence of himself and his use of the house as proper
for a gentleman and dynast (note the chorus' response, 569). The
ironic use is first made explicit in Admetus' statement to Heracles
that the dead woman was not a member of the family, but was
nevertheless ἀναγκαία δόμοις [essential to the house] (533). Finally
the contrast in attitudes, once established, is put to dramatic use
in Admetus' return from the funeral. There Admetus studies the
house very carefully, and concerns himself with domestic problems
(note the dirty floor, 946-947), realizing now that he is father and
mother (*cf.* 377-378). And he addresses the house in new terms along
with the old ones, as part of the suggestion in that scene that he
may be seeing things in a new light (862-863, 912-914, 941-950). But
interspersed is the ironic commentary (865-867, 882-888, 903-910,
935-940) which suggests rightly that Admetus' change and development are likely to come to nothing.

The use of the house and of the attitudes about it which are
both complements and contraries, is too extensive to sum up
briefly. It is a part of everything in the play. But for the ironic
structure the contrast is what is crucial: the quality of Alcestis' and
Admetus' concerns for the house is reflected in the quality of their
behaviour. Alcestis shows a loyalty to the household as a whole,
even to its lowliest members. She is capable of sacrifice. Admetus,
gentleman and dynast, maintains his magnanimity and his idea of
the house at the cost of personal ignobility and illiberality.

The third theme, death and its meaning, also develops on a
series of contrasts. Each character's response to the fact of death
serves as a focus for the playwright's interpretation of his other
characteristics. The attitude of the myth itself is explored through
imagery and through the character Thanatos, an attitude which is
amended and corrected by the ironic view.

The drunken Heracles delivers a speech on life's meaning for the
benefit of the outraged servant: "Do you know the nature of mortal
affairs? I think not. Where would you learn? Well hear me. Every
man must die. No mortal knows whether he will be alive tomor-

row" (780-784). Heracles, in his cups, speaks like a drinking song:
eat, drink, love, for tomorrow we may be dead. That every man
must die, and can never know how or when, is a commonplace often
repeated, since we never cease to be surprised that it is so. Here,
however, the commonplace has extraordinary piquancy because
Alcestis deals with a man who was an exception to that common
lot. Heracles argues that, since death is inevitable, the very un-
certainty of the time when it will come forces us to pay attention
to life, an argument that allows many interpretations, from those
of Sarpedon and Achilles in the *Iliad* to that of Trimalchio. Heracles' hedonism here has as its immediate conclusion "come have a
drink with me" (794-796), and Euripides uses the fact of his drunken-
ness throughout the scene (note his confidence that he will find
Thanatos drinking beside the grave, 845). But in Heracles' second
speech (837-860) Euripides also manages to suggest that other side of
hedonism, the heroic view of death celebrated in the *Iliad*.

Alcestis is brave but passive. She sees death as an alternative
which circumstances may make desirable, although "nothing is
more valuable than life" (152 ff., 244 ff., esp. 280-303). Her death
scene is presented twice, first by the maidservant who acts as a
messenger, later by dramatic representation. The reason why the
normal order is reversed and the report of the death scene precedes its dramatization is shown by the differences between the two
versions. The first introduces Alcestis and her emotions to the
audience, though the audience does not see her. The second introduces her husband and gives the audience a close look at him in the
light of what they already know about Alcestis.

Though Alcestis has a clear vision of Death, Admetus never sees
anything clearly, particularly necessities. He blames the gods for her
undeserved death, begs Alcestis not to betray him by dying, and
dramatizes himself and his grief with such inappropriate statements
as "stand up," and "your death is worse than death to me." It is not
Admetus who says that nothing is more valuable than life, but
Admetus cannot conceive of actually facing death. Admetus seems
unaware of the situation that is clear to everyone else. His own
death is never real to him, his wife's death barely. Shortly after
her death Admetus describes for Heracles the condition of Alcestis:
"Dead and not dead. She troubles me" (521). But six lines later
she troubles him no longer: "One who is going to die is already
dead, and the dead is non-existent," a mocking echo of Alcestis'
prediction a few moments earlier that she would be forgotten, since
the dead are nothing (381). "To be and not to be are considered two

different things," says Heracles (528), anticipating his later speeches.

Besides being presented as an idea in the minds of the characters, which can vary widely, Death is a character in his own right: a nervous bully who is afraid of a fight (29-40), a grotesque bogey out of a fairy-tale. Through the body of the play death is treated more seriously, but the fairy-tale character from the prologue is recalled for the final scene as the victim of a wrestling match.

Most of the functional imagery in *Alcestis* is related to death and resurrection, ideas which are seldom out of the minds of any of the characters. Central to the imagery of death is the "voyage of death," which is used as the counterpart of the common poetic image of the voyage of life. The river Styx is the counterpart of the "sea of life" (91, 112, 124, 213, 252, 263, 610). Death is a journey, and has its counterpart in the mystical journey of resurrection, of which the prototype is Orpheus' journey to retrieve Eurydice. Admetus, apologetic that he has not the voice of Orpheus, bans the lyre from his house also. Apollo, who saved Admetus, is associated in the imagery with Orpheus. Finally the journey of Heracles to retrieve Alcestis is compared with Orpheus' journey (213, 357 ff., 570, 610, 850 ff.). Apollo's son Asclepius, the other figure who resurrected the dead before Zeus forebade it finally, is invoked and mourned. Death is a disease which the medicine of Apollo and Asclepius can no longer cure (203, 236, 4, 121 ff., 135, 1047). Running through the imagery, from the argument between white-robed Apollo and black-robed Thanatos, is a play and alternation between black and white, dark and light, hope and despair. The forces of light and of darkness are wrestling for Alcestis in the melodramatic plot. Tension in that plot is underlined by the play of light and dark, and interpreted by the imagery of death and resurrection.

The symbolic expression of the tension in the plot is opposition between that certain journey into darkness which all must take, and that possible journey of resurrection for which one can hope. Apollo, Orpheus, and Asclepius offer some support to the hope. Zeus, Thanatos, and Ananke [Necessity] oppose it.

In the final stasimon the chorus recapitulates the imagery of the play, and resolves the tension by rejecting finally any hope for resurrection. Says the chorus: neither religion, in the form of Orphism, nor philosophy, nor poetry, nor the art of the Asclepiadai and Apollo can offer a comforting solution to the problem of death. Necessity keeps no altars and listens to no prayers. It is the will of Zeus and nature. But still there is some comfort: the necessity of death is balanced by the possibility of making life meaningful. The chorus suggests that Admetus take comfort in the fact that though Alcestis is dead and will never return, still she has a hero's grave, and her nobility will bring her honour like that of the gods. Travellers by her tomb will invoke her as a blessed daimon.

It is important to note what Euripides is doing with this final ode. Like Sophocles in *Antigone* (1115-1154) and *Oedipus Tyrannus* (1086-1109) he is establishing a mood and anticipation that are in direct contrast to the following denouement. Ignorance of the possibilities of the situation leads the chorus to a false hope in Sophocles' plays, and to a dismissal of one kind of hope in *Alcestis*. Since the audience, in all three plays, has heard a prediction of the outcome, its response to the denouement is sharpened by the dramatic irony involved. In Sophocles' plays the hope increases the impact of the tragedy. In *Alcestis,* just before the melodramatic plot reaches its climax the characters must view the situation as tragic.

⌈Euripides has also another structural purpose in reassessing at this point in the play the themes and imagery of death, and so in establishing an intellectual context for the final scene. To this point the play has suggested the results of various attitudes toward death. Admetus has denied life any meaning in order to stay alive, as he himself has just realized (960). Heracles faces his obligations and his own death (499-506) and feels himself free to enjoy life without remorse (773-802): "For solemn men with knitted brows life is not life, but misfortune." The final stasimon expresses beautifully and effectively what Alcestis' acceptance of death has meant: the chorus begins with a prayer to πότνια Ἀνάγκη [Lady Necessity] (976), but ends with an address to the noble and blessed Alcestis, transferring the term πότνια [Lady] to her (1004). Nobility in life and a hero's grave are an answer to death, and there is no other. This is a tragic view of death, and it calls forth some of the purest poetry of the play. It creates the context in which the audience is to view the final scene, a context ripe for irony. ⌉

The Testing of Admetus

Plot, the most important element of structure, remains to be discussed. Beginning with a very simple plot, which he announces in the prologue, Euripides spends the greater part of the play in variations on that plot. As one anticipates the plot from Apollo's prediction to Thanatos, the struggle of Admetus' family against death is to be brought to success at the last moment through the appar-

ently incidental act of entertaining Heracles. Alcestis is to be saved
from death's clutches and restored to her husband. But when the
hero Heracles does appear, just as Alcestis has died, he is not even
told about her. First there is a casual conversation with the chorus.
Then Admetus' lie prevents Heracles from finding out about her
death as the audience expects him to. The funeral follows, and
the audience is left in some perplexity about Apollo's prediction.
When Heracles reappears it is only after he has been described as
drunk and disorderly. Yet he leaves the stage with the purpose of
saving Alcestis, and perhaps he leaves the audience with the impression that he does not know what he is doing. Between the two
appearances of Heracles, Pheres attacks the moral basis of the
melodramatic plot while the corpse offers evidence. In these ways
the melodramatic plot is delayed for suspense, humour, and criticism.

[A second, ironic, plot structure, coordinate with the first, is introduced subtly at first as a theme, but gradually more prominently
until it is dramatized in the final scene as the plot itself. That is the
testing of Admetus.

> διπλῆν φοβοῦμαι μέμψιν, ἔκ τε δημοτῶν,
> μή τίς μ᾽ ἐλέγξῃ τὴν ἐμὴν εὐεργέτιν
> προδόντ᾽ ἐν ἄλλης δεμνίοις πίτνειν νέας,
> καὶ τῆς θανούσης.   1057-1060

[I fear two kinds of reproach, for my
citizens who might test me and find
me wanting because I betrayed my
benefactress and fell into the bed of
another young woman, and the reproach of the dead.]

In these terms Admetus describes his situation in the final scene, as
he refuses to accept the unknown but attractive girl who will witness
the sequel. There is a verbal reminiscence of Apollo's description of
Admetus' canvassing for a substitute (πάντας δ᾽ ἐλέγξας [testing
everyone] 15) and of Admetus' words to his father on the same subject, as he accuses Pheres of baseness, cowardice, and betrayal:
ἔδειξας εἰς ἔλεγχον ἐξελθὼν ὃς εἶ [when you were put to the test you
showed what you are] (640). The metaphor is general, that is,
it is never tied to the idea of touchstone, law-court, or the like.
Admetus has tested his family and found them ignoble, and found
that they betrayed him. Admetus himself, since his first entrance,
has faced a rather indefinite test in each scene: whether honour

forbids the entertainment of Heracles under the circumstances (551-567); whether to reject his parents and his own birth in the name of Alcestis as he rejects Pheres' gift to her (629-641); and whether, after the funeral, he can keep his vow, be master and mistress in the house, and face the women and men of Pherae (935-961). The issues have never been clearly drawn—honouring or betraying his wife is never as clear and simple as it seemed at the moment of her death (note 371-374). But in the final scene Admetus sees and describes himself as brought definitively to the test and forced to prove his quality, and to prove to his subjects and to Alcestis that he is no traitor.]

The situation, however, is ambiguous. For Heracles, who has shown his own nobility and can speak ἐλευθέρως [freely], there is no indication that the situation represents a test at all. On the contrary, for Heracles the scene begins as good natured, though perhaps not too tasteful teasing, which is spoiled when his noble host turns out unexpectedly to be stuffy. This scene is a formal parallel to the first Heracles-Admetus scene. In the first, Admetus lied to Heracles, while Heracles protested, for form's sake, against eating and drinking in a bereaved house. Here Heracles lies to Admetus, and assumes that Admetus, protesting for form's sake, will be convinced as easily. There is no indication in the text that Heracles sees any moral problem in the present situation or in the previous situation, beyond the fact that Admetus had discounted the friendship which Heracles is now proving (1010-1018). Heracles' concerns are not the same as those of either Admetus or the audience, since he was not a witness at Alcestis' death. Instead, all that Heracles says is in concert with his good nature and with the philosophy of life he has expressed previously: fulfill your obligations, live fully, and don't make life a misfortune. When Admetus refuses the girl and insists on seeing a moral issue where Heracles sees none, Heracles tries to save his joke by playing on Admetus' present sensitivity about women, which Heracles may suspect from the response of Admetus to the unknown girl (1061 ff.), but which the audience knows also from the previous scene.[13] In short, Heracles, who conducts the test of Admetus, is not aware of its implications, but can-

---

[13] Since his return from the funeral Admetus has been worrying about the difficulty of keeping his vows (911-925, 950-953). His emphasis on the difficulties of celibacy for the young (1049-1054, *cf.* 1085) recalls Alcestis' pathetic emphasis on her own youth (289, 316, *cf.* 471) which was echoed in the argument with Pheres (698, 711). It is not accidental that Euripides has Admetus give a detailed description of the status of the girl if she should be admitted into the house (1051 ff.). His speech prepares the audience for the betrayal.

not allow himself to lose the exchange, since it *is* Alcestis that he has
with him. He must either discard his joke or patch it up when his
host is unresponsive.

But for Admetus, the chorus, and the audience, the test exists and
has significance. Admetus makes that clear for himself in the lines
quoted above, though he still deceives Heracles by not mentioning
his vow to the dying Alcestis. Admetus' sensitivity here is a further
sign of progress after his insensitivity to the problems raised by the
chorus and male slave, not to mention Pheres (551 ff., 764 ff.).
Admetus made three promises to his dying wife, who had solicited
a single promise. And the audience is aware that in some sense
Admetus has broken, or allowed to be broken, the first two promises
regarding music and revels, by insisting that Heracles accept entertainment (*cf.* 343 ff., 425 ff., 751 ff.). No item in the promises or in
their breaking was quite definite, because nothing is quite as
Admetus foresaw it when he dramatized his own grief at his wife's
death. And since, to get Heracles into the house, Admetus offered
the technicality that Alcestis herself was not of his blood, not φίλος
but ὀθνεῖος or θυραῖος, and since this scene is a formal parallel to
that, the audience is invited to conclude that his important promise
to Alcestis, the one she solicited, will be broken, but somehow fulfilled by a technicality. For example the woman, if accepted as a
concubine, would not be a νύμφη Θεσσαλίς [a marriageable Thessalian girl], nor need she call Admetus "husband" or "bridgegroom"
exactly (328 ff., 1094). This is the ending suggested by the previous
parallel scene, and by the ironic treatment of Admetus.⌋

But an alternative ending has been suggested as well. Apollo's
prediction is fulfilled by the entrance of Heracles and the veiled
Alcestis, and this new movement in the final scene is something one
could not have anticipated as part of the melodramatic plot. Nevertheless even here, where the question is no longer "Will Alcestis be
rescued as predicted?" but "What are to be the conditions of her
restoration?", the melodramatic atmosphere of the play has suggested a sequel by insisting that virtue is generally or always rewarded, and that if Admetus is virtuous, he will be rewarded (note
9-10, 569 ff., esp. 604-605, and 837 ff.). Combined with the sugges-
tions of Admetus' increasing awareness in the previous scene, this
gives an expected ending: Admetus will pass the test and receive his
wife as a reward. His character and honour will be resurrected along
with Alcestis, and his rather shallow conversion ἄρτι μανθάνω [now
I realize] (940) will be turned into a profound one (note again ἄρτι
γεύομαι [now I taste this bitter grief], 1069). ⌊In the final scene, then,

Euripides puts both his structures to use, and creates a tension between the ironic plot, whose expected end is betrayal with a justification by technicality, and the melodramatic plot which would
demonstrate the reward of virtue.⟩

The scene begins on one note, and ends on the other. Admetus
himself raises the moral issue of which the audience has been conscious for some time. And he refuses to solve his problem by invok-
ing technicalities. His promise was a promise of celibacy, he says
(1090), and to accept the woman would be to break the promise,
would in short be the ultimate betrayal. "May I die if I betray her,"
says Admetus, rising to the occasion (1096). That the woman reminds him of his wife makes the issue clearer, and makes his emotions more touching (1061-1069). Admetus begins to pass the test
and again appeals to that sympathy in the audience which the irony
has dissipated. For one hundred lines of brisk argument, until the
middle of line 1106, Admetus retains his new strength of character.
He fights off appeals to his loneliness and to his habits of hospitality,
repulsing the attack on his honour. He even rises superior to what
Alcestis had predicted of him (with 1085-1086, *cf.* 381; with his
refusal throughout, *cf.* 181-182). When in 1104-1105 the argument
reaches what sounds like the final exchange, it appears that Admetus
has truly won over himself and his playful, unwitting opponent.
But at the moment of his anticipated victory Admetus suddenly
reverts to his more familiar character, and despite what he has said
he accepts the unknown girl:

> Αδ. καλῶς ἔλεξας· ἡ γυνὴ δ'ἀπελθέτω.
> Ηρ. ἄπεισιν, εἰ χρή· πρῶτα δ'εἰ χρεὼν ἄθρει.
> Αδ. χρή, σοῦ γε μὴ μέλλοντος ὀργαίνειν ἐμοί.
> Ηρ. εἰδώς τι κἀγὼ τήνδ' ἔχω προθυμίαν.
> Αδ. νίκα νυν.   (1104-1108)

Ad.   Your argument is well turned, but let the girl depart.
Her. She will, if she must. But first inspect whether she should.
Ad.   She must. Unless you are going to be angry at me.
Her. It is because of something I know that I want this.
Ad.   Have your victory, then.

Heracles has the victory, but does not know what he has won. The
following exchange (1108-1119) simply negotiates the terms of sur-
render. Heracles forces Admetus to take the girl himself rather than
hand her over to a servant. Admetus shows his delicacy by not
looking at the girl as he reaches out to take hold of her.

⌊Thus Euripides stages the test of Admetus. The spectators at first are led to expect that the restoration of Alcestis is to depend on a show of virtue by Admetus. And by a fine stroke Euripides arranges that the restoration itself is the test. At the crucial moment Admetus fails the test. He reaches out blindly for the unknown woman and in the act of betraying his wife receives her back. Euripides does not labour his point in the short and one-sided reunion between Admetus and his silent bride. The ironic themes are fulfilled, and as the tag added by the chorus insists, the incredible happens. Death is defeated. The reward of virtue goes to Admetus.

The irony is a sour sauce for the happy conclusion. Euripides dramatizes a betrayal, but the characters ignore it. He offers a resurrection, but does so by summoning again the fairy-tale Thanatos and by ignoring the tragic view of death to which he gave the ring of truth a moment before. The play's thematic material has suggested an evaluation of the myth in terms of honour, of human relationships, and the quality of life as conditioned by attitudes toward death, but of that evaluation nothing appears at the conclusion. The inference is left to the audience.

Euripides' irony is not gentle. Neither is it vicious or bitter. Or if there is bitterness in the play it is not to be found in the treatment of the person Admetus, who is weak, who fails his wife, but who is human and wants to live. We are led to understand Admetus, and so cannot scorn him easily. What is bitter, if anything, is the failure itself, and the dislocation of values that Euripides describes. Perhaps there is scorn of the myth and its tacit injunction to put one's faith in the unexpected, the unrealistic.⌋

Euripides' *Alcestis*

by D. M. Jones

The following notes do not pretend to be a complete treatment of the *Alcestis*. They have the limited aim of stressing certain features of dramatic importance in the composition of the play.

1. *The Fairy-tale Element*

The plot of the *Alcestis* is recognized as being in origin a fairy-tale rather than a heroic tale, one of the many variants on the theme of the cheating of Death by human cleverness, piety, or love. In the fairy-tale two worlds on different levels are brought into contact with each other. . . . Euripides chose to develop the human side of the story. The fairy-tale element could not be allowed to dominate and determine the sequence of human action and emotion of which Euripides wished to make the plot of his play. To reconcile the two worlds of the story so as to prevent the non-human element from awkwardly intruding into the human tale and making it absurd was the delicate task he had to accomplish; and the result shows, not that the fairy-tale element was an inconvenience to him, but that it was something which properly used could enhance the value of the play, just as misapplied it could have ruined it.

At the outset Euripides was helped in reconciling the two elements of the story by the local setting of the tale itself, and he shows the artist's characteristic skill in turning to account possibilities offered by the material. Thessaly was a land associated with magic, and Euripides keeps the Thessalian setting before our eyes. In 425-31 we are reminded of the Thessalian horses and of the magnificence of the courts kept by the Thessalian princes. In 588-

"Euripides' Alcestis" by D. M. Jones. From The Classical Review, *LXII (1948), 50-55. Copyright 1948 by The Clarendon Press, Oxford. Reprinted by permission of the publisher in a slightly abbreviated form and without notes. Some passages in Greek appear only in English translation (supplied by Editor).*

96 the Chorus sings of the sheep-rearing Thessalian plains, with
Lake Boebe and the surrounding wooded hills. In their first encounter with Heracles (476-80) the men of Pherae speak of their
ἄστυ [city], which to the visitor from the *polis*-regions of southern
Greece had seemed more to deserve the name of κώμη [village]. Admetus himself is represented in important characteristics as typically
Thessalian: he is a great landowner and stock-raiser and has the
Thessalian pride in hospitality, while Pheres' first answer to his
son's insulting language is that he is a Thessalian and sprung from
a Thessalian (677-8). Thessaly was a country in which wonders were
in place, and it serves Euripides as Tibet or Ireland might serve a
modern writer who wished to make use of a "supernatural" element
in his story.

In the structure of the play the two worlds are reconciled by being
to some extent kept apart, by the fact that their points of contact are
limited. Before seeing how this is done, we must note that in order
to support the fairy-tale element, that is, the saving of Admetus by
Alcestis and of Alcestis by Heracles, Euripides has used the common
device of introducing parallel myths. Thus, within the bounds assigned to it, the value and significance of this element of the story
are increased. The myth of Apollo as hired labourer (1 ff., 569 ff.)
gives a kind of historical setting to the story and develops the theme
of Admetus' piety and hospitality. The theme of the cheating of
Death is supported by the myths of Asclepius' raising of the dead
(3-4, 122 ff., 969-72) and of the saving of Admetus by Apollo (9-14,
32-3, etc.). Further, these myths are not merely parallels to the
saving of Alcestis by Heracles but are stages in the chain of events
leading to it. A similar pair of supporting myths are those which
have the theme of 'love stronger than death'—the stories of Orpheus
(357-9) and of Protesilaus; the latter Euripides could not use directly,
since in the chronology of the heroic age it came after the story of
Admetus, but he cleverly alludes to it by making Admetus say that
he will cherish an image of his dead wife (348 ff.).

The fairy-tale element provides the material for the prologue, including the dialogue between Apollo and Death. Death is here no
allegorical or philosophical figure, but the character of folk-lore
who lays hands on those whose life is forfeit and carries them off,
like the Charos who

> σέρνει τοὺς νεοὺς ἀπὸ μπροστά, τοὺς γέροντες κατόπι.

> [carries off the young in front, the old behind.]

The prologue introduces all the supporting myths except those of
Orpheus and Protesilaus, which are, as will be seen, specially relevant
to Admetus, and therefore come in his farewell speech to his wife.
The myths then disappear from the iambics, but are recalled in
lyric passages (cited above); the figure of Death, together with that
of Charon, returns in the delirious vision of Alcestis (252-6, 259-63),
which thus provides a kind of modulation from one plane to the
other. On the human level her vision can be satisfactorily accounted
for as due to delirium, as, indeed, her quick return to sanity indicates; she dies "in the full possession of her faculties." But remembering the prologue the audience is justified in feeling an added
thrill as though at the presence of an unseen and supernatural
power. To the two worlds of the story, then, are assigned the
different levels which the structure of a Greek play makes available
—to the fairy-tale world the prologue and the lyrics, together with
the hallucination of a mind at the point of death, and to the development of the human story the iambic dialogue and some of the
lyric passages.

In what manner do the two worlds influence one another? To the
undeveloped fairy-story both are equally necessary and on equal
terms. This treatment of the story is, in the *Alcestis,* mainly reserved
for those parts of the play assigned, as we have seen, to the folk-tale
element. In the human part of the story everything has human
motives and takes a human course, so that we might almost speak
of a "predetermined harmony." The arrival of Heracles and the
saving of Alcestis are foretold by Apollo to Death (64-9). But when
in the course of the play Heracles does arrive he gives for his
coming a humanly sufficient reason which has nothing to do with
the happenings at Pherae, and it is by accident that he learns of
Alcestis' death. This use of accident has offended some critics, and
it has been suggested that the manner in which Heracles learns of
the death of Alcestis is due to an oversight on Euripides' part. Euripides, however, like many other writers, knew that accident as well
as character has its place in a human story, and further, in the
Alcestis the accidents, as they seem from the human level, are provided for, or at least foreseen, on the supernatural.

One event on the fairy-tale level could not be treated as supporting myth—the saving of Alcestis. A messenger-speech describing the
events at the tomb would have ruined the balance between the
two elements which the rest of the play establishes. Euripides saves
it by taking advantage of the dual character of Heracles. In his

intercourse with mortals he is shown in what we may call his human-heroic character, speaking in a strangely matter-of-fact way even of his labours (e.g. 481, 483). In the same tone he mentions to Admetus his fight with Death. To secure this aspect of his character Euripides imparts to it a discreet admixture of the Heracles burlesqued in comedy. But in the speech where he announces his intention to save Alcestis (837-60), while the stage is empty of merely human characters, it is the divine-heroic side of his character which is prominent. Euripides thus reduces mention of the fight with Death to three lines in the human context, and dwells on it only when the absence of the Chorus and the human characters permits a second "modulation" by means of the person of Heracles to the non-human level.

2. *The Enlightening of Admetus*

In the composition of the *Alcestis* Euripides has made constant use of a device by which words, expressions, and ideas are first given prominence and are then introduced at a later stage of the action in a different and often more significant context. The examples of this technique, though the same in principle, vary in their working out, so that they produce no effect of monotony. This may best be illustrated by an examination of the means by which the attitude of Admetus is changed in the course of the play, and of the nature or content of that change.

The play in its human aspect presents a change of attitude, or an increase of enlightenment, in Admetus as the result of a series of emotional shocks. The death of Alcestis, with her farewell speech and the lamentation of the child, and the quarrel with Pheres are obviously to be regarded as shocks of this kind. The deception which Admetus is led to practise on Heracles is another. The serving-woman's paradox "You can call her both living and dead" (141), which from her had seemed pointless, even irritating, now reappears with horrible significance on the lips of Admetus (519 ff.): "I can tell a twofold story about her. . . . She is and is no more, a thing which grieves me." Each of these shocks produces no immediate change in Admetus, but is reflected at a later stage in the vocabulary of his utterances. Thus the bitterest moment of the deception of Heracles (532-3) is shown to have left its mark on Admetus' mind by the γυναῖκ' ὀθνείαν [woman not of our house] of 646; the words first used to mislead Heracles are now used in an attempt to shame Pheres. In the speech in which he attacks his father Admetus not

only uses ideas expressed by his wife in her last speech to him, but
also introduces, even in different contexts, a number of words which
come in a cluster in the speech of Alcestis. . . . Moreover, some of
Alcestis' arguments seem to have suggested points to Admetus. Her
criticism of Pheres and his mother for refusing to die for him he
takes over directly; compare 290-7 with 642-50. 651-2 have appeared
to some editors too obvious an echo of 295-6 to be genuine, but if
they are accepted, we have in Admetus' speech every gradation of
reminiscence from the verbal repetition of a particular argument to
the half-conscious or unconscious use of isolated words in different
contexts. In either case, the *verbal* material of 295 is taken up and
applied to Pheres in 650, so that the presence of Alcestis' words in
her husband's mind is not in doubt. In other cases, too, Admetus
adapts rather than borrows. Thus 653-4, where Admetus reminds
his father that his early life had been happy, seem to derive from
285-6, where Alcestis had described the happy life she might have
had if she had been willing to let Admetus die and herself marry
again. Alcestis had said in effect: "I might have had a prosperous life
if I had not chosen to die for you. If your parents had died in your
place, both you and I might have lived for the time remaining to
us." In the speech of Admetus the argument suggested by this is:
"You might well have died for me, for the time remaining to you
was short, and hitherto you have had a prosperous life." Again,
Alcestis' point in 293-4 that Admetus was an only child and that his
parents could not expect others suggested to him a number of arguments, for example 641, 655-7, and especially the cruel taunt in
662 ff.:

> τοιγὰρ φυτεύων παῖδας οὐκέτ' ἂν φθάνοις κ.τ.λ.

> [So you'd better hurry up and beget other children . . .]

The influence of Alcestis' speech on Admetus is shown in three
ways: by the arguments he takes directly from it, by the adaptation
he makes of other arguments from it, and by his use in a new
context of words and expressions suggested by it.

Admetus' quarrel with his father has seemed to many critics a
repulsive interlude. It is, indeed, shocking, and to no one more than
to Admetus himself. The fury of his onset shows the strain of mind
resulting from his wife's death and the unpleasant interview with
Heracles, and leaning on his wife's words he tries to throw off his
own uneasiness by a forthright attack on the selfishness of Pheres,
leading him to go beyond the bounds of decency in 662-5 when he

rejects his duty of giving his father burial; in this he is matched by
Pheres himself (726). What is the point of this, and why is Pheres so
unpleasant a character? In order to shake still further the emotional
compromise he had reached in the early part of the play, Admetus is
subjected to this miserable quarrel with one who is near and should
be dear to him, in the course of which things are said on both sides
likely to offend the Greek or, indeed, any humane sensibility. He is
given for the first time an outside view of his own conduct, and,
worse still, the complacent and ignoble love of life which he sees
and censures in his father he eventually comes to find in himself.
Once again there is a lapse of time before the scene takes effect in
Admetus' mind; his last words to his father show no change of attitude, but his speech on returning from Alcestis' funeral, especially
954-61, is the outcome of the quarrel. Euripides does not present the
tame spectacle of Admetus immediately accepting an outside view of
his own conduct, but the almost tragic one of him fighting against
it and losing.]

   The repetitions noted hitherto have been due to the delayed action of emotional crises in Admetus' mind, with one exception: his
use in order to deceive Heracles of a paradox first introduced by the
serving-woman. Other repetitions of this latter type appear when
the nature of his enlightenment is considered. At the time of Alcestis'
death Admetus, for all his grief, acquiesces, and by the use of the
crassest irony in the words he gives to Admetus Euripides makes
clear the blindness of that acquiescence (cf. 273-9, 382, 386, 391).
As the serving-woman had put it to the Chorus (145), οὔπω τόδ' οἶδε
δεσπότης, πρὶν ἂν πάθῃ [the master won't realize it until he suffers it].
In the speech beginning at 935 Admetus has at last come to see that
it is possible *propter uitam uiuendi perdere causas,* and with the
ἄρτι μανθάνω [now I understand] of 940 comes an echo of the
serving-woman's words, uniting the two utterances in the wider
context of the παθεῖν μαθεῖν [knowledge through suffering] adage
and marking the beginning and the end of the process of enlightenment. Admetus not only sees with another's eyes his own conduct in
accepting Alcestis' sacrifice, but he sees Alcestis' true value to him,
and realizes that his own existence depends on her life, not, as he
had thought, on her death. The remarks of the Chorus and of the
servants about Alcestis have often been treated together as Euripides'
expedient for exhibiting the character of Alcestis. In fact the view-
point of the Chorus is quite different from that of the servants. The
men of Pherae take the same attitude to Alcestis as Pheres and as
Admetus in his earlier mood; they praise her nobility and unselfish-

ness and lament with their king in his misfortune. The serving-woman and the attendant, on the other hand, emphasize the devotion of the servants to their mistress (192-5, 769-71), since they see the part she has played in Admetus' home. In his speech on returning from the tomb Admetus shows that he too has come to see Alcestis from this point of view, and has learnt the truth of his son's cry (414-15):

οἰχομένας δὲ σοῦ, μᾶτερ, ὄλωλεν οἶκος.

[Now you have gone, mother, the house is ruined.]

The words in which he anticipates the cold welcome that awaits him in his home are those with which the serving-woman had described the warmth of the servants' farewell to their mistress:

Admetus (941-2)

πῶς γὰρ δόμων τῶνδ' εἰσόδους ἀνέξομαι,
τίν' ἂν προσειπών, τοῦ δὲ προσρηθεὶς ὕπο]

[How can I bear to enter this house?
Whom shall I speak to? Who will speak
to me?]

Serving-woman (194-5)

κοὔτις ἦν οὕτω κακὸς
ὅν οὐ προσεῖπε καὶ προσερρήθη πάλιν.

[. . . and there was no one so lowly whom she did not speak to and was not spoken to in turn.]

The speeches of the serving-woman have a preparatory function not only in the obvious way of setting forth the circumstances at the outset of the action, but also because at three points of importance in the play her words come back with different and greater significance in the speeches of Admetus. This again, seen from the standpoint of the human action, is accidental, and on that very account the more effective.

3. *The Hospitality of Admetus*

How is the saving of Alcestis related to the change of attitude and to the character of Admetus? Is it to be taken as a mere accident, and her restoration to her husband as nothing but a pretext for exhibit-

ing Admetus in a happy situation which we feel he has now de-
served or at least can appreciate? Here again Euripides makes use
of the mythical side of the story. The myth of Apollo the hired
labourer which opens the play sets before us the only characteristic
of Admetus on which any stress is laid, his hospitality and righteous-
ness. The myth is taken up by the Chorus in the song which follows
the entry of Heracles into Admetus' house (568 ff.) with explicit
reference to the hospitality and nobility of Admetus, and marks
their whole-hearted acceptance of his defense of his conduct towards his guest. His hospitality prevents him from revealing Alcestis'
death to Heracles, and yet is indirectly a cause of its revelation, for
it leads to Heracles' unintentional provocation of the servant. This
virtue is insisted on to the end. The trick by which Alcestis is restored to her husband is not only entertaining in itself; it provides
a further test of the piety of Admetus both to his guest and to the
last behests of the wife whom he still thinks dead. Heracles takes his
leave of Admetus with the words (1147-9):

> Admetus, go on being just and pious in your treatment of guests.
> Farewell . . .

And by declining for the present Admetus' request (1151):

> Stay with us and share our hearth.

Admetus has, as a permanent part of his character, that which, in
spite of anything he does in the course of the action, wins the good-
will of the powers that can for a time suspend the demands of
Death, and in this he resembles Orpheus, whose power he envies in
357 ff., and Laodamia, to whom Euripides intends a reference in
348 ff. Thus within the bounds of the play is justified the belief of
the Chorus expressed at the end of the song in which, at a turning-
point in the action, they celebrate the hospitality of Admetus (604-5):

> My heart is fully confident
> that a god-fearing man will do well.

The Chorus and Admetus

by Thomas G. Rosenmeyer

How does an ordinary human being protect himself against too keen an awareness of the weight of necessity? How does he manage to save his self-respect in the face of predictability? By embracing the conventions, if we are to believe the *Alcestis*. Conventions are man-made, they give an illusion of human mastery, they afford a fixed point, a dignified rest in the toss of the errant cause. The instrument which Euripides employs to dramatize man's reliance on the conventions is, naturally, the chorus. Throughout the repertory of Greek drama the chorus has the role of affirming conventional morality and conventional perspectives in the face of heroic deviations from the norm. Often its conventionality appears to us more like triteness or stupidity. But its traditional stand provides an ever-present internal rectification of the heroic imbalance, a constant therapy of the heroic madness. In the *Alcestis* there are no heroes who deviate from the norm, there is no inkling of the grand madness or intransigence which we associate with the character of a Medea or an Ajax. Still, the chorus delivers its sermons. But now these pledges to convention do not have their usual counteractive force. Rather, they give us the essence of the chorus, and through them the essence of all men.

As soon as the choristers enter, they ask, in effect (79): "Are we to grieve or not? Somebody please tell us whether Alcestis has died or not!" For the people, it requires a ceremonial to cope with necessity. Their reaction to the fact of death is a matter of timing and ritual observance. Their mourning need not be any less heartfelt for being mechanized; but they guard well against its being spontaneous. The question of the chorus: What shall we do? is a nontragic dis-

"The Chorus and Admetus" (editor's title) *by Thomas G. Rosenmeyer. Section IV (pp. 217-23) of "Alcestis: Character and Death," in* The Masks of Tragedy: Essays on Six Greek Dramas *(Austin: University of Texas Press, 1963). Copyright 1963 by Thomas G. Rosenmeyer. Reprinted by permission of the author and publisher.*

tortion of the tragic dilemma expressed in the words: What am I to
do? In the *Alcestis,* the question really means: What does etiquette
require us to do? Or better: How soon may we fall back on the regu-
lations of etiquette? This is how the comedy of manners reformu-
lates the question of how one behaves in the presence of death. The
men of the chorus make no bones about it—they would be more comfortable if the Queen were already dead. They would rather practice the ceremonial than wait for it. At the moment they are waiting
for the conventional signs of mourning, for the groaning and la-
menting and beating of hands on breasts (86). In their mind's eye
they contemplate the vision of a beautifully appointed funeral, complete with bowl of water and curl of hair (96). They want Alcestis
dead so they can go through the apotropaic motions of the ritual.
But, being decent and generous, they are ashamed of their secret
expectations; they catch themselves and sing (90):

> Healer God, appear and soothe
> the wave of disaster!

as if Apollo had anything to say in the matter. But then again, later,
they turn to the servant girl and ask with an unhealthy but quite
natural eagerness (146),

> You're sure there is no hope she will be saved?

And again (150),

> Her death will make her famous!

In the eyes of the chorus, at any rate, Alcestis' death *is* a fact, and
they are impatient to get on with it.

Eventually, when the Queen has deigned to give up the ghost,
they remark, quite literally (416):

> You must, Admetus, try to bear this sorrow.
> You're not the first, nor will you be the last,
> to lose a worthy wife. After all, we must
> all of us go at one time or another.

This reminds us of nothing so much as of the Marx Brothers in
Room Service exclaiming pious inanities at a fictitious deathbed.
Would the effect in Greek be similarly funny? Perhaps not; it is the
traditional function of the chorus to express collective wisdom.
What seems silly to us, appears in many instances to have been intended as a serious contribution to the soothing of distress. Yet I
for one cannot see Euripides writing these lines without tongue in

cheek. For the chorus to say to Admetus "We've all got to go!" is comical in any language. The chorus relies on its stable conventions to see them through the present unhappiness, and they wish to let others share in this protection. They do not seem to realize that their age-old comfort cannot possibly be a comfort to their king.]

A second characteristic of the chorus spotlighted by Euripides is their strong sense of masculine prerogative. Apart from an initial reference (82) to "Alcestis, child of Pelias," the chorus refuses to consider the Queen in her own right, preferring to think of her as the wife of Admetus. At one point (220) they pray to Apollo to save Admetus from being hurt through her death. What matters is not her sacrifice but her husband's suffering (cf. 144, 199, 226, 241). Alcestis must die, that is her obligation and her fate; any feeling that may be provoked by this fate is to be poured into sympathy with the lonely survivor. It is his loss, not hers, which feeds the compassion of the chorus. In the eyes of the servant girl, on the other hand, it is Alcestis who merits the greater share of the grief; as for Admetus, he could have prevented the unhappiness (197):

> If he had died, that would be all. But since
> he ran from death, he'll have his torture with him
> always.

The chorus, manly and middle-aged, cannot appreciate the greatness of the Queen's decision or, later, the violence of her suffering; they can speak and feel only with other men. They are too old-fashioned to put themselves in the place of a woman, too simple to look at the situation from two points of view. As in the original folk tale, Alcestis is for them little more than a means to an end, a willing instrument to ensure the survival of the King. For the slave girl, Alcestis is a heroine, and Admetus a coward.

[Euripides is playing fast and loose with traditional morality. Tyrtaeus, the spokesman of masculine virtue, had said: "The man who deserts his post will lead an outcast's life, and in the end he is going to die anyway; hence, face death, for so you will live gloriously, or earn glory in death." In our play this creed is, with but one significant change—eternal pain instead of eternal shame—enunciated by the slave girl, while the brave men of the chorus, loyal supporters and spiritual companions of the King, throw the dictates of heroism to the winds. They seem to think that the privileges of their sex and the continued survival of masculine power should cancel out the claims of manly courage and *arete*.]

What kind of a person is this man who is willing to sacrifice his

wife? First of all let us look at the tradition. An ancient drinking
song advises as follows:

> Friend, learn the rule of Admetus and keep distinguished company.
> Keep away from the mob; there is no grace in them.

In the old songs, apparently, Admetus was the ideal aristocrat, gracious, class-conscious, cultured to his finger tips, the kind of prince
whose self-righteousness is unshaken by irrelevant notions of charity
or brotherly love. In the folk tale on which the play is based, his
superior standing guaranteed him a hero's rank, and he achieved
the hero's supreme authentication by, for a time, overcoming death.
That his wife got lost in the shuffle was unfortunate and regrettable
but justified by the results. He was invincible, and she was one of
his means of defense. In retrospect the victor has a right to expend
fortifications. The brilliance of his position induces us to regard the
death of Alcestis a mere incident and to forget it.

In Euripides' play Admetus is still the gracious and refined gentleman, but though his royal power is great (588), his personal distance
from his subjects is much reduced. Like most of Euripides' kings, he
is actually a man of the people, more sensitive perhaps than the rest,
but a little confused and not entirely happy in the elevated position
in which fortune has placed him. More important, Euripides shifts
the emphasis of the ancient tale; he concentrates less on the deed
itself than on the implications and consequences of the deed. He
asks the question: What happened to the wife, and could the King
really stand by and see his wife die for him without a stir of embarrassment? It is as if a dramatist were to take up the story of
Hansel and Gretel and ask: What precisely was the position of the
witch? Did she suffer? Could the children who caused her death
sleep the sleep of the innocent thereafter?

[Because of the new light thrown on Alcestis, we are now made to
see Admetus from a radically different angle. It is the servant girl
who supplies us with the fresh perspective: Admetus is a fugitive
from justice, with Apollo, the god of blue-blooded honor and re-
finement, aiding and abetting him to turn tail. Worse yet, Admetus
implores his wife not to "betray" him. He uses the word on more
than one occasion (e.g., 250, 275). The servant girl copies the usage
in her report (201):

> He weeps and clasps his lady in his arms
> and begs her: "Don't betray me," . . .

Admetus falls back on the same word to characterize his parents' un-
willingness to die for him (659). It is a military term, taken straight
from the spiritual arsenal of Tyrtaeus and other writers of patriotic
poetry. Strictly speaking, it is applicable only to Admetus himself
and no one else. We wince to hear it used of one who is a very
much better soldier than he. But as a piece of psychological portrai-
ture it is perfect. Admetus has transferred his fate to the shoulders of
Alcestis; she is about to die, there is nothing now he can do to head
off the event, and he is beginning to resent this infraction of his freedom to will and act. At the peak of his frustration he persuades
himself that she is dying of her own free choice, and that she rather
than he is the one who could yet rectify the mistake. There is some
justice in this. The whole dramatic treatment does conspire to make
Alcestis appear a freer agent than her husband. Admetus expressed
a wish, and the gods acted; Alcestis had no gods assisting her to
facilitate or direct her choice. Hence Admetus blames Alcestis for
not revoking her decision.

The absurdity and the violence of his entreaties suggest that he
is not without his share of tenderness. A coarser man might have
commiserated with the woman, and yet taken the situation in his
stride. He is vulnerable, hence he suffers. Again and again he assures
Alcestis of his love and his concern. When he says to her (277): "If
you die, we [he includes the children] shall die too," he means what
he says, however preposterous the sentiment. He treats his wife as an
equal, as a cherished partner in life. He wished to escape death, and
he allowed Alcestis to substitute for him. But all that, Euripides
wisely saw to it, is part of the antecedents, part of the folk tale rather
than the drama. The facts are fixed, the drama cannot change them,
it can only study the consequences of the facts. Seen from this
vantage point, the sorrow of Admetus is not an ignoble thing. When
the chorus, prior to the actual death of Alcestis, pity Admetus and
voice their fear (328) that his suffering might drive him to suicide,
we are at first inclined to feel that their compassion is misdirected.
But they are right; his suffering is intense, and he knows that death
might well have been better than the prospect that is now before
him.⌉

⌈His personal embarrassment is that he cannot translate wish or
thought into action. His life is a prime example of the ordinary
man's incapacity to live the life which Aristotle recommends, the life
of choice and commitment, the heroic life. He recognizes the sordid-
ness of his existence, but he cannot lift himself above it. We are

tempted to look down on him, but we should know that the figure of Admetus is a mirror in which we may recognize ourselves. The image is not repulsive, but it leaves little scope for pride or moral satisfaction, in spite of the honesty with which Admetus comes in the end to admit his inadequacies. The *Alcestis* inspires little pity, and less fear, but, in spite of the humor, a humiliating sense of solidarity.

Heracles and Pheres

by Thomas G. Rosenmeyer

In T. S. Eliot's *Cocktail Party* the Stranger says to Edward:

> Most of the time we take ourselves for granted,
> As we have to, and live on a little knowledge
> About ourselves as we were. Who are you now?
> You don't know any more than I do,
> But rather less. You are nothing but a set
> Of obsolete responses. The one thing to do
> Is to do nothing. Wait.

Admetus has waited because he took himself for granted. But this cannot go on in the light of the new fact, the emptiness where formerly he could count on a life beside him. We expect the recoil. But before we come to the awakening of Admetus, Euripides transforms the whole mood of the action by the introduction of a new character. Again let me quote from the *Cocktail Party*:

> Just when she'd arranged a cocktail party.
> She'd gone when I came in, this afternoon.

Whereupon the unidentified guest says:

> This is an occasion.
> May I take another drink?

Before very long we shall see Hercules take that drink. Now he arrives, and his fast-paced interview with the chorus completely cuts off our preoccupation with death and frustration. This is the start of something new, a breath of fresh air admitted into the dank

prison house of blindness and inaction and, above all, of pretended
purposefulness.

Hercules happens to pass by on his way to perform his eighth
labor, the taming of the fierce horses of Diomedes. He has recently
completed the seventh, the overcoming of the Cretan bull. He has no
exalted view of his duty; unlike Admetus he does not regard his
position in life as a basis for speculation and bargaining. As the
slave of Eurystheus he has a certain job to do, and that is that.
Though a servant, he faces death repeatedly, as Admetus, the master
of Apollo, cannot. Hercules is content to risk death even in a matter
which is of no concern to him. From the manner of his talk about the
horses of Diomedes it is quite apparent that he has no interest in
them either as adversaries or as commercial value. What is more, he
has not been briefed about them. Admetus, homo contemplativus,
has all the insight and acumen he needs to appraise his situation
properly, but he tries to shut the knowledge out until it can no
longer be blinked. Hercules, homo activus, is truly uninformed; he
undertakes each labor as if it were a business requiring nothing more
than mechanical action. His matter-of-factness leaves no room for
insights or fears or beliefs. The greatest hero of Greek fairy tales—
and here Euripides once more has his fun with us—is not imaginative enough to believe in fairy tales. The man who is going to take
the personal existence of Death seriously enough to wrestle with him
and choke his windpipe, refuses to credit the existence of supernatural things. When the chorus suggest that it will not be easy to
tame the horses of Diomedes, he replies tolerantly (493):

> Surely they don't breathe fire from their nostrils?

Of course every child in the audience knew that that was precisely
what the wild Thracian horses did do. Hercules just has a good laugh
at the notion and goes about his business, pretending not to like it
(499),

> Just my tough luck! I always get the worst breaks!

but eager enough to carry out the mission all the same. Hercules is
not involved in the tragedy of inaction which plagues Admetus and
his people. Nor is his role in life dependent on the support and com-
forts extended by fellow men. Admetus, even at the moment of his
self-discovery and conversion, could not cope with his lot unless he
knew himself to be a member of the group, sharing with them his
anxieties and his dreams. Hercules stands alone; his simple strength
and uncomplicated outlook operate best without the softening influ-

ence of human bonds. Nor again is he weighed down by conventions; being a successful man of action he has no need for them. He is in every way uninvolved. And the absence of involvement is dramatized visually through a break with the traditions of the Greek theater: his scene with the steward is played on an empty stage, with the chorus gone to attend the funeral.

Hercules is not entangled in the meshes of the errant cause; his cause is freedom, the freedom of spirit and freedom of action. Freedom is the theme of a drinking song which he bawls out, much to the pious horror of the steward. As corroborated in the speech which follows, the theme is pedestrian and untragic: Drink and be merry, for tomorrow you will die (782). With the Herculean labors freshly engraved in our minds, there is considerable humor in the spectacle of the Stoic saint preaching the philosophy of Omar Khayyám. Surely he is the one man in the world who does not pursue a hedonistic career. And yet, the man of action easily turns into the clown; Hercules' freedom from involvement also places him beyond the restrictions of a meaningful commitment. He does not need to be sensitive or tactful or morally obligated; he stands by himself, above the claims of society. It is perhaps worth noting that Euripides is here engineering a clever scheme of deflection. In the literary tradition it is Admetus who was associated with the philosophy now offered by Hercules. A poem by Bacchylides, who lived a generation or so before Euripides, contains these lines:

> The lord Apollo
> . . . spoke to the son of Pheres:
> "You are mortal; hence you shall foster
> two thoughts, that you will see no more
> than the light of tomorrow's sun,
> or that you will draw out and complete
> a deep-treasured life of fifty years to come.
> Then, do what is right and enjoy yourself;
> that is the greatest of all profits."

In Euripides' version Admetus cannot take life so lightly; his friend Hercules can, and he can exemplify the finer qualities of Admetus to boot: warmth, generosity, tolerance.

Unlike the chorus, Hercules sees only kindness, not extravagance, in the fact that Admetus entertained him without informing him of the true conditions. In spite of his servile status he can admire a good act without envy or resentment (855):

He took me into his house, he did not drive
me away, despite the fierce weight of his sorrow;
he hid it, in his kindliness and with
his usual tact. Is there in Thessaly,
or Greece, a man more liberal than he?

Hercules is a man without bitterness, without aggressions; he has no
privileges to safeguard, no fancied status to maintain. His eye is free
and unclouded, his heart ready to be moved by the actions of his
friends. He may be somewhat lacking in imagination, but his
capacity to love and admire is unlimited.

Why does Admetus deceive Hercules? For one thing, to admit that
Alcestis had died would have meant provoking awkward questions.
Hercules knows of Alcestis' promise, but the accomplished fact would
force him to regard Admetus in a different light. Hercules does not
believe that she will die—he does not believe in fairy tales—and so
Admetus feels himself safe from his contempt. To this extent Admetus' silence is selfish, a further token of his lack of fiber. The
chorus are appalled at his silence, but for another reason. In their
eyes, admitting Hercules into the house is a breach of the conventions, or rather the breach of one convention in the interest of another, and they doubt that the duty of hospitality could ever take
precedence over the duty of mourning. But that is exactly what Admetus seems to feel; a true Thessalian, raised in the traditions of the
frontier and the wide-open spaces, he regards the duty of entertaining a guest as canceling all other obligations.

But that is not all; in effect, Admetus is trying to take the easy
way out. Upon Hercules' question whether his wife has died (518),
he answers: she has, and she has not. The whole passage which follows is riddling, and Hercules has a point when he remarks: "You
are talking mysteries!" Riddling is a kind of ritual; by reducing the
status of Alcestis and his own lamentable part in the affair to the
terms of a conundrum, Admetus hopes to be able to live with his
guilt more easily. Hercules is less subtle, he has no taste for puzzles,
and asks to be excused (544): "Let me go!" he says, using the words
which Alcestis had used at the moment of her vision of Charon. Admetus allowed Alcestis to leave him; he cannot now allow Hercules
to do likewise. Hospitality is easier to exercise than marital obligation. It is a beneficent convention, ordered to measure to help you
forget the sting of personal defeat. Admetus craves to salvage what
is left of his pride, by clinging to the embarrassed guest. The tenacity

with which he presses him is an index of his desperation. It leads him
to renounce even the last shred of his moral integrity (541):

> The dead are dead; come, go into the house!

Coming from the delicate Admetus, this is indeed a callous pro-
nouncement. He is attempting to escape, both from his own remorse
and from the painful memory of his wife's last actions. But the
escape into the role of host, even if momentarily effective, cannot
last. The time must come when Admetus will recognize his delusion
and struggle to rid himself of it.]

At this point the chorus, apparently forgetful of their earlier criticism of Admetus' conduct, sing their second great choral ode, a
hymn to hospitality (569), in rhythms usually reserved for the ex-
tolling of victorious kings or athletes. The ode, with its praise of
Apollo—an earlier guest who should never have come in the first
place, and who stayed too long when he did—is designed to create
an impression of security and contentment. The language is pastoral;
the emphasis is on peace, stability, simple pleasure, the happy life.
The song starts with an address to the house, then turns to call upon
Apollo, who is pictured, like Orpheus, attracting the animals with
his lyre (thus adding to the number of the house guests), and settles
down to describe the wealth and liberality of Admetus. These three
—the house, Apollo, and Admetus—form a compound image in
which the meaning of hospitality takes concrete shape. True hospitality is the willed expression of a life that is full, happy, relaxed.
At least it should be that. But often it becomes a gadget employed to
make it appear *as if* the life which occasions it were unimpaired. In
our play, hospitality is the most impressive manifestation of the
code which is the ordinary man's support in the stream of life, and
which marks its practitioner as a civilized person. But there is no
doubt that it is mainly for the weak. They are the hosts; the strong
are guests.

⌊Hospitality, Admetus briefly hopes, will allow him to find his
moorings. But the record of the convention as it pertains to this tale
does not leave much room for confidence. The hospitality tendered
by Admetus to Apollo initiated the loss of Alcestis. Admetus entertains Hercules, wrongly in most people's eyes, but the *faux pas* starts
her recovery. Finally Admetus tries to shake off his weakness and proposes to deny hospitality to the mystery woman, and almost loses
his wife once more. Thus the code, in its conflict with genuine sorrow and genuine involvement, makes for some difficult situations.

But nothing better can be expected from the slipshod tactics of the civilized man who lives by rules rather than by instinct. Once the manipulation of the code has been substituted for the life of courage and conviction, the control must slip from the hands of the agent.

*   *   *

There is a man in the play whose instincts, it seems, are as simple and straightforward, though not so generous, as those of Hercules: Pheres. It is true that when he comes on the stage he has a perfectly respectable little speech, full of pious and acceptable sentiments. One might almost believe that he is not an interested party, and that the reports about him put out by Alcestis were not entirely accurate. But this impression is at once wiped out when we come to the last two lines of his opening remarks, where he reveals his real feelings with singular coarseness (627):

> This is the sort of marriage that turns to profit;
> otherwise marriage is not worth a straw.

The method is characteristically Euripidean; neither Aeschylus nor the pre-Euripidean Sophocles has it (though Homer does): a man betraying his secret thoughts in an unexpected final disclosure, an epigrammatic revelation of the self, as if the pretended sentiments got to be too burdensome for the speaker to maintain. His remark immediately puts us out of sympathy with him, and makes us accept the position of Admetus in the scene which follows with less revulsion than might otherwise have been the case. And yet we cannot help but admire the old man; unlike his son he has not talked himself into believing his own fictions. He can take or leave the code as it fits his purposes, his true instincts always being on hand to run their consistently unsentimental course.

Admetus, to be sure, behaves like a cad. He calls his father a coward (642, 717), apparently forgetting his own inglorious role. Taking a leaf from his father's book he addresses him in terms of law rather than affection, as if the relationship between father and son were little more than a legal contract which might be revoked at the signer's discretion. The effect of his inaction has been to destroy his judgment and to atrophy his humaneness; for a brief interval he dispenses with his gentlemanly ideals of kindness and good will. His father repays him in kind. From legalistic charges and countercharges—I disown you, I have a new father and mother! . . . What crime have I committed? Have I stolen from you?—the quarrel degenerates into a battle of insults, into the most vitriolic enactment of the war of generations in Greek drama. No punches are pulled as the young calls the old superannuated, and the old, with equal justification, sneers at the softness and the dishonesty of the young.

Pheres says that he has no understanding of the nature of Alcestis' sacrifice (728):

> *She's* pure and blameless, yes; but does she have sense?

⌐While Admetus decries his parents for the purpose of magnifying Alcestis, Pheres cannot see any point to her deed. He prides himself on being levelheaded, unromantic, unconfused; he does not mind being coarse in the bargain so long as the truth as he sees it comes out into the open. His coarseness is painful but it has a function. For it exercises on Admetus a peculiar spell which helps us to understand him further, and which eventually helps him to understand himself. Goaded by the memory of his wife's not-so-silent reproaches, angered by his father's brutal cynicism, the gentle Admetus turns savage and fanatical. The explosion is as terrible as it is unexpected. It must lead either to destruction or to catharsis. And this gives us a clue concerning the role of Pheres in the plot. His own character is drawn vividly enough; but his appearance in the play is due chiefly to the fact that Euripides is interested in the soul of Admetus, in the experience which a good man undergoes when faced with the fact of a loved one's death. ⌐

One barb which Pheres uses in his scolding is particularly sharp; he calls Admetus *sophos*—clever, or ingenious (699). Admetus is that. To say that you expect your parents to die for you is immorally clever; to consider such a statement natural, as Admetus in his violence does, is downright sophistical. But "cleverness" does not quite meet the situation, for Admetus is, at this stage, too confused to merit the tag. In reality his *sophia* is fantasy, self-delusion. A good son is made bad, his filial responses are distorted, by a good deed which put him to shame. The explosion helps to untwist the responses and to transmute the fantasy into a *sophia* proper, into an insight into his true self. ⌐Pheres functions as a kind of psychotherapist to assist Admetus in his recovery from the wound which Alcestis has dealt. That is not to say that Pheres thinks of himself as a healer; he is too old and too crude to think of anyone's welfare but his own. But he operates as one nonetheless. His refusal to participate in the fiction which his son has elaborated for himself shocks Admetus into first compounding and then surrendering his fantasy, into turning from delusion to knowledge. Pheres is little

more than an instrument, a tool of conversion. After the scene between father and son, there is no further mention of Pheres; he has
done the job he was designed to do. And when Admetus comes back
from the funeral he is a different person.]

Not so the chorus; they have changed very little, continuing to
rely on their double props of convention and masculinity (892): it
happens all the time, you are not the first one to lose a wife, and so
forth. They do not understand the new single-mindedness of Admetus' grief, and on one occasion they offer a veiled criticism (903):

> I had a kinsman
> who lost a son, an only son;
> his death was bitter
> cause for tears. Nevertheless,
> he bore the loss well, though childless now,
> and graying of hair,
> and closing in on the eve of life.

In other words: too much fuss over a dead wife.[But Admetus can
no longer, after the set-to with Pheres, take shelter in externalizing
or ritualizing his guilt. He begins by addressing the house, once the
symbol of fullness and contentment. Now he is reluctant to enter it
because it reminds him of the emptiness in his life and the draining
away of his own self (861):

> Hated entrance way, hated sight
> of an empty home! Where am I
> to walk, where to stand? . . .
> I have been ill-starred from birth.

Apollo has enriched the house, now he has impoverished it; and Admetus has begun to realize that he is not separate from the house; as
the house goes, so goes he. He had been blind to believe that life,
domestic and political—as the second choral ode shows, the house
symbolizes both—could go on much as before; that, with Alcestis
gone from his side, he could continue to exercise his function as
father and king. The delusion is gone, and Admetus recognizes his
guilt.

In his speech after the musical exchange which marks the second
entry of the chorus, Admetus openly confesses himself at fault. He
does so by using the only formulation then readily available to a
man and citizen. He imagines outsiders and personal enemies pointing their fingers at him and whispering (955):

> There goes the man who lives in shame, who did
> not dare to die, who bought a coward's life
> with his own wife's death . . .
> who hates his parents for his own panic!

And the capping humiliation:

> Is he a man?

The formulation is in terms of what anthropologists call shame rather than guilt; the language of guilt was not yet easily handled by Euripides or his audience. But the self-questioning of Admetus clearly is a pregnant dramatization of the dawning of guilt upon a soul in the process of conversion. "He has turned tail before Hades; is he a man?" Greek tragedy of the grand genre, the tragedy of Oedipus or Medea or Prometheus, does not allow for a learning from experience or a wisdom through suffering. But Greek melodrama, or tragicomedy, or the sort of drama we have here, occasionally does show us a hero who recognizes his faults and suffers for them and learns from them. Conversion is not a tragic business, it does not rouse the emotions of which Aristotle speaks. But for an author who is interested in character and character development, conversion is an eminently desirable theme. In the story of Admetus, Euripides gently guides us through the career of a man who, though initially self-deceived, proves his worth by permitting himself to be shocked into an admission of his cowardice. He now sees himself with the eyes of Pheres; and that is the beginning of his restoration to favor with the audience.

The Happy Ending of *Alcestis*

by Kurt von Fritz

. . . The question then arises of how we can understand the ending of Euripides' tragedy, if Admetus doesn't deserve the return of his wife from the kingdom of the dead (which, after all, forms the end of the play) either through his omnipotent hospitality or through his repentance or some other deep change of heart. At this point we must say once and for all that none of the notorious endings of Euripides' tragedies, in which a *deus ex machina* appears at the end and cuts the knot which cannot be untied and with one stroke resolves everything to the satisfaction of all, can be taken seriously. (In this play Heracles functions as a *deus ex machina,* even though, unlike the *dei ex machina* in many of the later plays, he does not confine his appearance to the end but also plays an important role in the rest of the drama.) Superficially the purpose of these endings is to bring one back to the traditional story. But the fact that the poet was "bound to the received version of the story" could hardly be the main reason for their appearance, as most critics, even including Verrall, assert. Departures from a traditional version are not infrequent either in Euripides or his predecessors. But whenever, with the help of a *deus ex machina,* he "adds on" (I use the expression deliberately) an artificial happy ending, the contrast between the "idealistic" optimism of the tale and the cutting realism with which the poet treats the mythical situation in the main body of the play becomes far stronger than if he had altered the traditional ending.

To give a detailed justification of this conception of the *deus ex machina* in all the plays of Euripides would demand a separate

"The Happy Ending of Alcestis" *(editor's title) by Kurt von Fritz. From* "Euripides' 'Alkestis' *und ihre modernen Nachahmer und Kritiker,"* in Antike und moderne Tragödie, neun Abhandlungen *(Berlin: Walter de Gruyter and Co., 1962), pp. 312-16. Copyright 1962 by Walter de Gruyter and Co. (formerly G. J. Göschen'sche Verlagshandlung). Translated by John R. Wilson. Reprinted by permission of the publisher.*

study. Here we can briefly explore only two aspects of the problem. Observe first that when Euripides uses the *deus ex machina* in his late plays, he makes the unreality of these happy solutions increasingly obvious. An extreme is reached in *Orestes,* where the hero stands for at least 80 lines holding a dagger at the throat of Hermione, the daughter of his uncle Menelaus, and threatens to kill her, although she has done him no harm. At last the *deus ex machina,* in this case Apollo, appears and explains to him that he is destined by fate to marry the girl "at whose throat you are holding a dagger" (1653). Eighteen lines later Orestes finally lays aside the dagger with the words: "See, I am letting Hermione go unslaughtered" (1671), and states that he agrees to the marriage that has been decreed by fate "if her father gives approval." At this the father not only unhesitatingly approves the marriage, but even expresses his satisfaction that such a noble young couple should be joined in the bonds of marriage.

This "happy" ending of an Orestes tragedy is the very embodiment of bitter mockery. Euripides seems to have despaired at the general public's refusal to understand the meaning of the unexpected happy endings to so many of his tragedies; and this time he wanted to make his meaning blatantly clear, though even here, as later commentaries to *Orestes* show, he was not altogether successful. But quite apart from the grotesque element of the Orestes-Hermione scene, consider that in *Electra* Euripides had done everything to visualize the horror of matricide, regardless of the circumstances under which it had been committed, and at the end of that play had made the Dioscuri in their capacity as *dei ex machina* sharply criticize Apollo for having commanded Orestes to do it. How in *Orestes* could he have seriously thought that all that was needed to set everything right again was for this very same god Apollo to appear and make arrangements for a marriage and other acts of atonement?

Admittedly in *Alcestis,* as in all of Euripides' earlier plays which end happily, the unreality of such an ending is more delicately hinted at than in the work of his last decade. An indication of this unreality is the fact that Alcestis remains dumb and untouchable till the end of the play. Although Heracles proclaims that this need last only three days—that is, until she has loosened her ties with the world below, under whose influence she had already fallen—this only thinly disguises the impossibility, after what has happened, of the wife's simply falling into the arms of her husband and continuing to love him as though everything were normal. For what else could Euripides have put at the end except some banal thoughts about the happiness of reunion? This would certainly not have harmonized with the tragic character of the play, which depends precisely on the break between the married couple being more than physical. Or he could have put an exact counterpart of the death scene, in which it would become very clear that nothing had really changed in the relationship which had come to light between the married couple, i.e. on Admetus' side love was always present only as a form of *penia* [poverty], of need for the other, never, as with Alcestis, in the form of *poros* [abundance]. But Euripides is not writing any Ibsenesque Nora scene, quite apart from the fact that the ironic depth of the transposition of a fairy tale into reality would have been spoiled. Or else, to use the expression so often found at the end of a Dostoevsky novel, he would really have had to begin "quite another story," a story which Euripides obviously did not intend to write, and which Dostoevsky for obvious reasons actually never did write. *So we come to the simple realization that, just as Euripides starts out from a fairy tale, so he returns to it at the end, after he has shown in all the intervening part of the play what happens to the tale when it is transposed into reality.*

It is true (and this is our second point) that this conception of the role of a *deus ex machina* in Euripides generally, and of the happy ending of *Alcestis* in particular, might seem to go back, though in a different way, to the assumption (for which Verrall has been criticized) that one must first solve a riddle to understand a play by Euripides and feel the effect intended by the poet. But this is not so, for by saying that the happy endings introduced by the *dei ex machina* cannot be taken seriously, I do not mean that the person understands a Euripidean play best who says to himself when a *deus ex machina* appears: "There is no such *deus ex machina* in real life. Actually Orestes would have been stoned and Alcestis would have stayed in the grave." On the contrary, it is quite irrelevant whether or not Euripides believed in the real life appearance of *dei ex machina*. In the play their entrance just as much as the arrangements they make should be taken as real by the audience. Otherwise the whole effect of profound irony in these endings would be lost. But the happy endings which such *dei ex machina* bring about are not at all happy, as *Orestes* patently makes clear. For can anyone believe that the marriage between Orestes and Hermione can be very happy after Orestes had wanted to kill her merely to hurt his uncle, though Hermione had done nothing to harm him?

Once we see this, and understand that Euripides undoubtedly intended it, the whole paradoxical effect of the ending of his plays is clarified. In one way or another every spectator has sensed that the happy ending of *Orestes* is grotesque and not really happy, and this is certainly true of those ancient and modern critics who criticize Euripides for bringing in a solution "in such an external and mechanical way." To this extent they have, without knowing it, understood him quite correctly. They have felt the shock which they should have felt. But at the same time they have also misunderstood him by criticizing the "external solution" and have altogether failed to see that this solution is really not external but, because life goes on, is basically more tragic, or of a tragic quality much more suited to Orestes as Euripides depicts him, than his death by stoning would have been. And yet it should be obvious that if Euripides had only wanted to disentangle the plot in any fashion and connect it with the traditional ending, he wouldn't have finished with such a grotesque scene as that between Hermione, Orestes, Apollo, and Menelaus.

In *Orestes* people have sensed and taken note of the shock of a happy ending which cannot be happy. Hence they have accused the poet of giving a mechanical end to his play, as though *he* had thought of the happy ending as happy. In *Alcestis* people have also felt the proper sense of shock and so in a certain way, through their unconscious emotions, understood the author. But they have taken the happy ending seriously and at the same time, since the poet has seen to it that this happy ending cannot possibly be justified by what precedes it, have either made a desperate attempt to reinterpret the play so that the happy ending can be real or, if they saw this was impossible, have duly criticized him for not knowing his business and tried to improve his play, with the curious but really quite natural result that on close inspection the improved versions are quite inferior to the original in form and effect.

We can say that *Alcestis* and *Orestes*, as well as other controversial plays by Euripides, are in a way understood by those who have misunderstood them. The mixture of enthusiastic admiration and strong criticism with which Euripides was received from the start indicates as much. For in this case it is not a matter of criticizing individual lapses or simply of a group of enthusiastic admirers *vs.* a group of severe critics. On the contrary, the whole history of Euripidean criticism and imitation shows that the most intelligent of his readers and audience are the very ones who are torn between admiration and antipathy. This is especially true of *Alcestis*. It is all due to the sharp discord which Euripides has struck in almost all of his plays, and which in many of them is also expressed in the bald discrepancy between the plot and the apparently happy ending. This effect shows that, as Euripides intended, the discord is also heard by those who cannot solve the riddle of why they are so deeply disturbed.

The Mute Alcestis

by Erna P. Trammell

Though many a scholar has been perplexed about the fact that after a certain point in Euripides' play of the same name Alcestis is mute, as yet no one has suggested a convincing solution why she is so. Certainly it is not because Euripides has to use for other purposes the actor who previously had been playing her part. Nor was her speechlessness a suddenly conceived device when at the end of the play he found himself confronted with the necessity of three rather than of two speakers. Her silence, we may be sure, means something. Throughout the play Euripides makes use of every opportunity to stress the dread of pollution innate in god as well as man. As early as verse 22 Apollo suggests leaving the home of Admetus before he is tainted by death. In Antistrophe I the elders call our attention to the fact that the cup of clear spring water, an antidote against death's taint, had not yet been placed in the gateway. When Admetus asks Heracles the reason for Alcestis' muteness he informs him, not in his usual bantering manner, but in all sincerity, that she must be "unconsecrated" to the powers below and that she may not speak "until the third day comes."

Nobody under a ban of pollution could address others until he had been purified. This custom is attested by the three great tragedians. In the *Eumenides*[1] we are told, "It is the law that he who is defiled by shedding blood is debarred all speech until the blood of a suckling victim shall purify him from murder." In *Oedipus Tyrannus*[2] the soothsayer rebukes Oedipus thus: "Thou alone did'st do the bloody deed. From this day on speak not to these or me. Thou art the accursed polluter of this land." The defiled Orestes tells Iphigenia how everyone avoided and shunned him: "Thither

"The Mute Alcestis" by Erna P. Trammell. From The Classical Journal, *XXXVII (1941-1942), 144-50. Reprinted by permission of the publisher.*

[1] Vs. 448.
[2] Vs. 350.

I came, but no guest-friend would at first welcome me as one ab-
horred of heaven. Some pitied me; yet my fare set they out on a
different table and by their silence banned me from all conversation." [3] Helen absolves herself as well as Electra from the curse of
pollution: "I consider myself unpolluted by thy speech since I lay
all the blame on Phoebus." [4] The frenzied Hercules is distressed
when he finds himself in much the same predicament as Orestes:
"Should I remain, what temple or religious ceremony would I
attend? For I am guilty of a crime that forbids my being spoken to." [5]

Divinity did not seemingly invest one with immunity from contamination with death. Even to the eternal gods it was a source of impu-
rity; so much so, that all the graves were removed from Delos in
order to make it sacred to Apollo,[6] and the dying were driven away
from the shrines of Aesculapius—this, though he himself was a
healer.[7] The priestess of Artemis protects herself and her goddess
by warning Orestes in no uncertain terms: "Artemis bars from her
temples and considers polluted anyone whose hand is stained by
the blood of man or who has touched a corpse." [8] In spite of their
omnipotence they could not escape the taint of death. They would
desert a friend in need to avoid it. Just as Apollo forsook Admetus in
order not to witness the death of Alcestis, so Artemis abandoned her
devotee in time of great need to insure her own personal safety:
"Farewell! I may not watch man's fleeting breath nor stain my eyes
with the effluence of death." [9] So fearful were the ancients of this
particular kind of infection that distance meant nothing. Plutarch
tells us that rites of purification were conducted for the living at
Argos when it was reported that fifteen hundred men had been lost.[10]

By the simple act of cutting a few hairs from the forehead Death
had consecrated Alcestis to the gods below. To absolve that con-
secration she must perform certain prescribed rites. Paley imagines that Alcestis will satisfy the claims which the nether gods have
upon her by expiatory and propitiatory rites; Monk, that she will
perform rites opposite in nature to those whereby she was consecrated. Woolsey is the only editor, however, who has any definite

[3] *Iph. T.* 947 f.
[4] *Or.* 75 f.
[5] *Her. Fur.* 1282-1284.
[6] Polybius VIII, 30 and Pausanias I, 43, 3.
[7] Pausanias II, 27, 1.
[8] *Iph. T.* 381-383.
[9] *Hipp.* 1437 f.
[10] *Praec. Ger. Reip.* XVII, 814 B.

idea how Alcestis was to sever her connection with Hades. He sees its solution in Plutarch's description of the manner in which one supposed dead rejoins the living. One of two methods he must pursue, either enter the house through the roof or undergo a ceremony symbolic of birth:

> If the returned is really a ghost or infected with the pollution of death in some way, his entrance by this route (i.e., roof) will not pave the way for the entering of death by the door; and if he is alive and well, the process will presumably do him no harm. At least it will not hurt the family.[11]

The precaution is prescribed not in the interest of the person returning but is enforced by relatives and probably for their protection. This may explain why the sick man referred to in Mark II, 1-4 was let down through the roof. Christ could more easily have performed his miracle out in the open, for the weather was fair if the assembled crowd is any criterion. On the other hand, he could have accomplished nothing if all the spectators had fled out of their fear of contamination. And so, since neither the superstition nor the remedy interfered with Christ's work, he passed it by without comment.

Pollution and contagion of death might also be neutralized by suffering rebirth:

> When a certain Aristinus realized that those for whom a funeral or burial had been held were considered unclean and could not mingle with people even in a temple, he went to Delos to learn from the attendants of Apollo what ritual he must follow. The Pythian oracle replied: "To reestablish yourself with the eternal gods you must cleanse yourself by the same rites as a woman purifies herself after childbirth."[12]

Wyttenbach includes in his comment on this passage a similar story by Hesychius: "When Polemon, who had been regarded as dead, was ordered not to enter the temple, he darted through the folds of a woman's dress, as this was symbolic among the Athenians of being born again." Wyttenbach compares this practice with the rite of adoption by simulated birth, and it is, indeed, apropos. By just such a ceremony as this did Heracles himself become the foster son of Hera and Zeus and was thereby elevated to the rank of the gods:

[11] Cf. H. J. Rose, *Roman Questions.*
[12] Plutarch, *R. Q.* 5.

Heracles mounted a couch and pressed close to Hera. She imitated
real birth by letting him fall to the floor from the folds of her robes.
This is exactly what the barbarians do when they wish to make
somebody their son.[13]

Simulation of birth is still practised among the Bulgarians, Bosnian
Turks, and Berawans. So in ancient Greece a man supposed er-
roneously to be dead was treated as dead by society until he had
gone through the ritual of being born again.

In ancient India, under similar circumstances, the supposed dead
man had to pass the first night after his return in a tub filled with a
mixture of fat and water. There he sat with doubled fists and without uttering a syllable, like a child in the womb, while over him
were performed all the sacraments that were wont to be celebrated
over a pregnant woman. The next morning he got out of the tub
and once more went through all the sacraments.[14]

Any number of religious sects make use of such a ceremony to
denote new life. The Orphic tablets allude to a similar practice:
"The initiate of the Orphic religion darts through the loose gar-
ment of the goddess of the underworld and is transformed into a
god." [15] In the Eleusinian mysteries we find an attempt at represent-
ing the return of Persephone to the upper world and to her mother.
Even to the initiates of that day the performance must have appeared a little ludicrous, to judge from the following excerpt: "Do
not laugh at the mysteries! Demeter is in travail, for Persephone is
being born again." [16] The method of regeneration among the
Hindus was slightly different, but the fundamental idea is one and
the same. They observed the tradition in spiritual rebirth. Three
days after a priest had laid his hand upon an initiate, he (i.e. priest)
was supposed to give birth to a Brahmin.[17] Through a baptism of
blood the devotee of Attis received new life, and to keep up the
fiction of a new birth the initiate lived on milk for some time.[18]
The ritual may undergo change from time to time, but the principle will ever be the same. The mystic rites, like Christian baptism,
symbolize not only the death of a past life but the birth of a new
one.[19]

[13] Diodorus Siculus IV, 40, 2.
[14] Frazer, *Golden Bough* I, 75.
[15] Olivieri, *Lamellae Aureae Orphicae:* Bonn (1915), 4.
[16] Clemens Alexandrinus, *Protr.* II, 14.
[17] Dieterich, *Mithrasliturgie:* Berlin (1910), 468.
[18] Frazer, *Adonis, Attis, and Osiris:* London (1906), 172.
[19] Eitrem, *Offeritus und Voropfer der Griechen und Römer:* Cristiania (1915),
99.

Only two of the many editors of the *Alcestis* offer a suggestion as to the possible significance of "until the third day comes." Jerram thinks the number three may be used because of its well-known mystic character, or that it is, perhaps, an allusion to the sacrifice made to the dead on the third day after the funeral, or even to the offering due the deity on the third day after the death. From the enumeration of funeral ceremonies given by Pollux[20] we do not know whether the "trita" was held on the same day as the burial or three days thereafter. Stengel is of the opinion that it took place on the same day as the burial and was preceded by three days of fasting, during which period the mourners were regarded as unclean.[21] The Roman rite of purification lasted three days and was followed by a banquet in honor of the dead.[22] The "trita" was every dead man's due and an obligation which an expectant heir had better not leave undone, for a corpse has been known to complain because he thought he was being cheated of it. Lysistrata, for example, in talking to the magistrate whom the women have dressed up like a corpse, remarks: "You complain because we are not laying you out? Don't worry! On the third day the funeral feast, prepared by our own hands, shall be ready for you." [23] This passage implies two things: first, the importance of the "trita"; and second, that Aristophanes sets it on the third day after death. Non-fulfilment of such a rite might mean the forfeiture of an inheritance. The expectant heir, you will remember, in proof of this contention that he was the adopted son and recognized successor of a certain Menecles, testifies: "I myself buried him and performed the 'trita' and the 'enata' i.e. the ninth-day sacrifice." [24]

It is my opinion that behind the belief in the presence of the dead at the "trita" [25] lies the assurance that not until that day did the body and soul actually part company, and that for this reason the third day has become the traditional day of resurrection. Hampered as he was by the three unities, Euripides had to content himself as well as his readers by stating that regeneration would require three days, or what Woolsey terms "the day but one after." Innumerable examples prove such to have been the popular belief. This is exactly the period of time that elapses in the sixth book of the

[20] I, 8, 146.
[21] *Die Griechischen Kultusaltertümer:* München (1898), 146.
[22] Aulus Gellius XVI, 4.
[23] *Lysistrata* 611.
[24] Isaeus, *Menecles* 27, 46.
[25] Aulus Gellius XVI, 4; Cicero, *De Leg.* II, 25, 63; Stengel, *Die Griechischen Kultusaltertümer,* 156.

Aeneid, in which Vergil illustrates concretely the doctrine of rebirth by the "katabasis" of his hero, Aeneas. Though this may be
a mere coincidence, yet investigation might prove that the same is
true of other "katabases." Our Lord, too, descended into hell and
on the third day rose again from the dead. Man, too, has been seemingly dead for the same period; for an Athenian, Cleonimus by
name, was so grief stricken and despondent upon witnessing the
death of an intimate friend that he swooned. After he had been
seemingly dead for three days, he was laid out according to the
law. As his wife was removing the raiment to anoint his corpse, she
detected a heavy breathing. Needless to say, the funeral, already
under way, was halted. Still another such incident is recorded by
Proclus:[26] "Rufus came back to life yesterday after he had been
dead three days. He says that he has been sent back by the gods
of the lower world to hold the games which had been promised his
people. After the fulfilment of his promise he must die again." The
popular belief that the soul of a man remains with his body for
a period of three days may be hinted at in the legend of the raising
of Lazarus: "Lord, by this time he stinketh; for he hath been dead
four days." We see that the possibility of restoring life to the dead
was accounted hopeless after the lapse of three days because by that
time corruption had set in. It is easy enough to see how this belief
won credence after the divine resurrection.

This idea is still made use of in ceremonies of regeneration. At
puberty the boys of the Javanese race are admitted to their native
association. The initiates are blindfolded and taken to a hut in the
thick of the forest to remain from five to nine days. With the disappearance of each boy within the enclosure "a dull chopping
sound is heard; terrible cries ring out and a sword or spear dripping
with blood is thrust through the roof. This is a token that the boy's
head has been cut off and that the devil has carried him away to
the lower world, there to regenerate and transform him." [27] Although the rites themselves last from five to nine days, the men
who act as sponsors return to the village on the third day to an-
nounce that the devil has restored the youths to life. "The faint-
ness and muddy attire of the messengers convey the assurance that
they have just returned from the lower world."

The above evidence substantiates my conviction that the phrase
"until the third day comes" does not specify the time required for
the ceremony or purification, but designates the traditional period

[26] *In Rem Publicam Platonis* 614, 2 ff.
[27] Frazer, *Golden Bough* 1, 696 f.

during which the soul itself knows not whether it is to abide by or desert the body. This three-day muteness of Alcestis was not a "clumsy device" to overcome the lack of a third actor, but a clever and ingenious invention to glorify her resurrection amidst the stillness of the tomb.

Alcestis and *The Cocktail Party*

by Robert B. Heilman

In revealing, in 1951, the affinity between his *Cocktail Party* and
Euripides' *Alcestis,* T. S. Eliot permitted himself a hint of triumph
that this relationship had not yet (two years after the first performance of the play) been detected. Mr. Eliot had had the very human
satisfaction of keeping his secret, and in keeping it he had incidentally insured that the immediate criticism of *The Cocktail Party*
would not be, like that of *The Family Reunion,* confused by ob-
servations upon its genealogy.

After the pleasure of keeping silent, there was the pleasure of
breaking silence and of proclaiming the unsuspected truth. But this
pleasure, with its legitimate histrionic ingredient, must have been
compounded by the fact that the hidden history now brought to
light was really not quite credible. Mr. Eliot admitted that it took
"detailed explanation" to convince his acquaintance of the "genu-
ineness of the inspiration." [1] For the public, his unelaborated assertion of the kinship remains almost shocking; surely one of the
minor Greek dramas, very much less than a tragedy though considerably more than a satyr play, seems the unlikeliest source for
a "sophisticated" contemporary play, with its dominant comedy of
manners, its intimation of tragedy, its reminiscences of parable,
and its ambiguity. The bafflingness which hangs over *The Cocktail
Party* is the least conspicuous trait of *Alcestis.* Nor did Eliot cushion
his shock by outlining parallels that would compel recognition and
assent. Rather his public statement had the effect of retaining, at
the moment of revelation, something of the mystery, for he noted
only a single resemblance—that of the eccentric guest who drinks
and sings. But in *The Cocktail Party* the Unidentified Guest's par-

---

"Alcestis *and* The Cocktail Party" *by Robert B. Heilman. From* Comparative
Literature, *V (1953), 105-16. Copyright 1953 by* Comparative Literature. *Reprinted by permission of the publisher.*

[1] T. S. Eliot, *Poetry and Drama* (Cambridge, Mass., 1951), pp. 38-39.

tiality to gin and song is so incidental that one is scarcely aware of it except at the level of theatrical gag; that it may have been suggested by Heracles' conduct at Admetus's palace is of no help whatsoever in assessing the serious role of Sir Henry Harcourt-Reilly. Perhaps Mr. Eliot believed that further elaboration would be uninteresting; or perhaps his tip was partly playful, embodying the incomplete confession of a devoted entertainer carrying a little further the theatrical game to which he had committed himself. Or there's another possibility; Mr. Eliot's apparent joke may be a pedagogical joke, and his meager clue to what he has done an invitation to seek out the heart of his performance.

About the intention of his announcement we need not speculate; but the fact is that to look at *The Cocktail Party* steadily in the light of *Alcestis* is to see some of its lineaments a little more clearly (and, conversely, the Eliot play provides a perspective from which one can discern potentialities, perhaps unsuspected, in the Euripides play). Again, one need not inquire into the formal intention of the playwright, which at best is likely to be more complex or fluid than some students of literature may be predisposed to admit or than the author himself may be aware—and which, as the work itself assumes autonomy, may undergo progressive and radical modifications until, in the end, the "intention" realized in the completed work may be quite different from the "intention" which presided over the first strokes of composition. We might say, for instance, that Eliot intended to "imitate" *Alcestis* or to write a "creative revision" (cf. Dryden's "regulative revision" of *Antony and Cleopatra*) or a "dramatic analogue" of it, but all of these formulations would be loose. I would rather say, going on the evidence of the plays, that *The Cocktail Party* seizes upon thematic material latent in *Alcestis* and dramatically explores it further, reinterprets it, and enlarges it. As Raymond Radiguet has said, "A creative writer runs no risk in 'copying' a work, since this is impossible to him. The creative mind will instinctively discard the model, and use it only as a fulcrum." [2]

Eliot may even have got a hint from the tone of *Alcestis* and then, as with theme and character, gone markedly beyond his original. *Alcestis* is, in our terms, romantic comedy; but its distinction lies in its almost daring flirtation with tragedy. From one point of view, Admetus is like a Molière butt; from another, he is almost the tragic hero—the "good man" with a flaw that leads to

[2] Quoted by Jean Cocteau in his Preface to Madame de La Fayette, *The Princess of Cleves*, trans. by H. Ashton (London, 1943), p. ix.

disaster, and with some capacity for self-recognition. Admetus comes
very close to the soul searching of an Oedipus or an Othello: "O
my friends, what then avails it that I live, if I must live in misery
and shame?" [3] But his facing of the situation he has brought about,
his facing of himself, his facing of guilt—all this is cut short by a
miraculous intervention which, in restoring Alcestis to him, accom-
plishes that adjustment of circumstance which is at the heart of
the comic mode. Eliot calls his play "a comedy," and in its wit, in its
agile use of incongruity, and in its espousal of accommodation as a
value its comic quality is plain. But Edward and Lavinia Chamber-
layne are both treated like Admetus in being compelled to undergo
moral introspection; indeed, theirs is very much more severe and
penetrating than his, and to that extent *The Cocktail Party* goes
further toward the tone of tragedy. Besides, there is Celia, who alone
of the dramatis personae is capable of living tragically. But her
derivation from *Alcestis,* if indeed she does derive from it, is a
problem of character to which we return later.

   The way in which Eliot has imaginatively worked out from *Alcestis* in his own direction will be most clear if we first notice the
parallels in plot, the anatomical resemblances, between the two
plays. These are astonishingly frequent. The action of *Alcestis* takes
place on the day on which Alcestis dies for Admetus, the action of
The Cocktail Party begins on the day Lavinia leaves Edward.
Admetus is grief-stricken, Edward is chagrined and even seriously
disturbed. However, Admetus is most hospitable to Heracles, and
Edward carries on with the cocktail party, trying to be a good host
to his guests. Admetus minimizes the seriousness of the situation by
concealing the fact that it is his wife who has died; likewise Edward
tries to pass off Lavinia's desertion as something less serious, a visit
to a sick aunt. By giving Edward not one but many guests to con-
tend with, Eliot has enlarged the social situation created for Admetus by the arrival of Heracles.

   But if Heracles in one sense becomes many guests, the parallel
between him and the Unidentified Guest is not given up but is
rather carefully elaborated. Heracles' arrival is unscheduled, the
Guest appears to have "crashed" the cocktail party. Immediately
on Heracles' arrival, his courage and resourcefulness are established
for us by his telling the Chorus about his adventures; as soon as
the Guest talks to Edward alone, he exhibits confidence and author-

---

[3] The Richard Aldington translation, in *Seven Famous Greek Plays,* ed.
Whitney J. Oates and Eugene O'Neill, Jr., Modern Library College Edition (New
York, 1950), p. 278.

ity. Heracles' questioning of Admetus is exactly paralleled by the Guest's blunt interrogation of Edward. As Eliot has told us, Heracles gets drunk and uproarious, and the Guest drinks and sings. The Servant reproves Heracles for his conduct; Julia mockingly reproaches Edward,

> You've been *drinking* together!
> So this is the kind of friend you have
> When Lavinia is out of the way! Who is he? [4]

Heracles promises to "bring back" [5] Alcestis to Admetus; the Guest, referring to Lavinia, uses the phrase, "If I bring her back," and then assures Edward, "In twenty-four hours/She will come to you here." [6] Heracles makes a game of urging Admetus to give up his grief and find consolation in a new marriage, and similarly the Guest enjoys pointing out to Edward the advantages of independence from his wife; both husbands, of course, want their wives back, and in each story the wife is brought back by the tormentor. Heracles' sudden unveiling of Alcestis is paralleled by Sir Henry's surprise confrontation of Edward and Lavinia in his office; although Lavinia has come back to Edward physically, Sir Henry now takes on the major task of restoring them to each other morally. And, to complete this catalogue of surface likenesses, Death has come literally to Admetus's palace to snatch Alcestis, a fact surely alluded to, humorously, in Julia's exclamation to the newly returned Lavinia, "Don't tell me you were abducted!" [7]

Eliot's variations are plain enough to dispose of any idle supposition that he is simply rephrasing, as it were, an original, just as the evident substance of his own work makes impossible a suspicion of mere virtuoso ingenuity. The ingenuity—even the virtuosity—is there, of course; but having in a sense paid tribute to it by noting the systematic affiliations of play to play, we need to go ahead and see what end it serves. Eliot's underlying performance is the perception and the amplification of certain meanings which inhere in Euripides' plot and characters—in the myth which he took over and in the skillful entertainment which he made of it. When Heracles, reproved by the Servant, makes a lively, imaged promise that he will leap upon Death, wrestle with him, wound him, and

[4] T. S. Eliot, *The Cocktail Party* (New York, 1950), p. 34. All references are to this edition.

[5] *Seven Plays*, p. 273.

[6] Page 33; cf. pp. 32, 109.

[7] Page 84.

compel him to yield up Alcestis, he gives us the background for the
Guest's sober statement to Edward: ". . . it is a serious matter/To
bring someone back from the dead." From the original action Eliot
has distilled an "idea" which he proceeds to work up. Edward replies:

>   From the dead?
> That figure of speech is somewhat . . . dramatic,
> As it was only yesterday that my wife left me.[8]

By "dramatic" Edward doubtless means theatrical, improbable—
a judgment that might almost seem to have point if we did not
see that the metaphor is drawn from the literal story in Euripides.
Now, since Eliot has said that he wished the origin of his plot to
remain unknown, the reinterpretation of a wife's dying for her
husband as a desertion of her husband may seem a dextrous trick
of concealment. But it is clearly more than a tour de force; rather,
Eliot is taking the literal story and uncovering its symbolic possibilities, or, in other terms, both naturalizing and universalizing the
folk mystery. The result—the definition of desertion as death, and,
by extension, of the rupture of the marriage as itself a death (rather
than, say, a convenience or a casual legality or quest for integrity)—
is to compel a reconsideration of the nature of the relationship of
Edward and Lavinia, that is of husbands and wives generally, and a
profounder sense of what it entails. Husbands and wives are "alive"
to each other when their relationship, even a halting one, goes on;
in this sense marriage itself is "life." But Eliot is not content to
halt at this recognition; he characteristically pushes on to the paradox that must be assimilated. The Guest replies to Edward:

> Ah, but we die to each other daily.
> What we know of other people
> Is only our memory of the moments
> During which we knew them.[9]

In the more obvious sense death is departure, separation, rupture;
but in a profounder sense, death is ever present, inevitable, the

---

[8] Page 71.

[9] Pp. 71-72. Several lesser details in this scene involve, despite the ironic
seriousness of tone, a kind of joking reminder of *Alcestis*. When Edward asks,
"So you want me to greet my wife as a stranger?" (p. 72), and the Guest pre-
scribes, "When you see your wife, you must ask no questions" (p. 73), we can
hardly fail to see a recasting of Euripides' final scene, in which the veiled
Alcestis is a "stranger" to Admetus and in which Admetus is told Alcestis must
preserve a three-day silence. The ritual requirement is translated into a psy-
chiatric stratagem.

unbridgeable separateness of men and women even in their most
intimate relationship. Marriage is life, but this life must be understood to include death. The doctrine does not propose despair,
however, but looks toward conquering the death of separation by
a reunion grounded in the acknowledgement of imperfect actuality.
Through "death" they gain not eternal, but temporal, life, which
must include something of death. This "moralizing" of the literal
death in Euripides is one source of the relative spaciousness of
Eliot's drama. Another source is Eliot's working out of the potentialities of Euripides' characters.

The treatment of Edward and Lavinia in Acts II and III of *The
Cocktail Party* leaves us with so strong a sense, first, of the need of
both of them to understand themselves and to work toward making
"the best of a bad job," as Edward calls it, and then, of their re-
ciprocal efforts to achieve what Reilly calls "a good life," that we
are likely to forget the situation in Act I, when the picture we are
given is not of a blowup caused by equal failure on both sides, but
of Lavinia's precipitating the break through motives which she at
least regards as generous and helpful. She tells Edward:

> I thought that if I died
> To you, I who had been only a ghost to you,
> You might be able to find the road back
> To a time when you were real—[10]

Again the double value of death: death as a breaking of their life,
and death as a concomitant of their life—though here, in Lavinia's
view, it has gone beyond the "normal" alienation of individuals
implied in the earlier speeches of Reilly (the Guest). In the fine
paradox of the "ghost" who can "die" Eliot has amplified the
Euripides story, just as he has subtly varied it by the minute change
of *die for* to *die to*. In granting to Lavinia an element of unselfish-
ness (and in this instance she is hardly to be read as a victim of
self-deception), Eliot retains the center of Alcestis's character, but at
the same time he alters the proportions. In Alcestis the over-all
emphasis is on the spirit of sacrifice, with the self-regarding emotions coming in secondly and secondarily—some self-righteousness,
some resentment against Admetus's parents, and a bargaining sense
and fondness for power which lead her to proscribe remarriage for
Admetus. In Lavinia we have only a glimpse of generosity, and see
her mainly (before the new self-discipline and insight of Act III)

[10] Pp. 97-98.

as an agile combatant in marriage, opposing her husband with a selfishness that complements his own, and with a managerial tendency derived from Alcestis but greatly expanded.

This change of proportions, however, is less important than another difference; Eliot has really seen two characters in Alcestis—the ordinary woman and the saint—and has boldly split Alcestis into Lavinia and Celia (whose name, we may suppose, is not an accident). On the face of it such a split looks like a reduction of one complex person (the woman not completely submerged in the nun, as Lowes said of Chaucer's Prioress) into two simpler ones—the housewife and the *religieuse*. But Eliot is very careful to leave neither wife nor saint at a level of allegorical simplicity. He endows Lavinia with some trace of the self-abnegatory and with a capacity for understanding herself and others and for feeling a general moral responsibility in the world—just as he compels Celia to earn her sainthood by the trial and error of an affair with Edward, by the "desperation" of a sense of aloneness and sin, and by the rigors of her "journey." The fact that he makes the split shows the influence of his belief upon the form of the materials in which his play originates; world and spirit are different realities, and must be represented in different dramatic actions (since Lavinia—and with her, Edward—is granted a kind of "salvation" within their ordinary, secular world, we can see Eliot's development from *The Family Reunion,* in which, so to speak, salvation was possible only to spirit and the world was simply condemned for not being spirit). As the possessor of a rare capacity for spiritual achievement, Celia appears in a dramatic movement which in effect reverses that of Alcestis. Alcestis has performed her great act of spirit before the play opens, and a considerable part of her own actions on the stage show her dwindling into a wife, whereas Celia grows, having to discover the inadequacy for her of the mere wifely, so to speak (she sees that she had created Edward, her lover and possible husband, out of her own aspiration), before she can make her great choice of the "second way." Yet at that it is remarkable how much of the Alcestis story remains in the treatment of Celia—for instance, the suffering and horror of the final experience, as both dramatists instinctively guard against the cloying effect of the Griselda motif. Alcestis cries out, "What a path must I travel,/O most hapless of women!" [11] and Reilly acknowledges to Celia "It is a terrifying journey" and says after her death,

[11] *Seven Plays,* p. 250.

I'd say she suffered all that we should suffer
In fear and pain and loathing—all those together—
And reluctance of the body to become a *thing*.
I'd say she suffered more, because more conscious
Than the rest of us. She paid the highest price
In suffering. That is part of the design.[12]

Euripides' story is virtually made for Christian readaptation—a human being dying that another may live and then rising from the dead. Eliot omits the resurrection, except symbolically, perhaps, in the impact of the Celia story on others, but he does heighten the Christian analogy by having Celia die by crucifixion. At this point, unfortunately, the drama of Celia has trailed off into an undramatic post mortem.[13]

Eliot has drawn heavily upon Admetus, not only in such details of the action as we have mentioned, but in the general outlines of the moral experience. As soon as Alcestis actually leaves him, Admetus begins to realize her value to him; he tells Heracles that he does not want another wife. Likewise Edward realizes his need for Lavinia and rejects Celia, whom now he might have. In fact, when Eliot makes Edward say both "I cannot live with her" and "I cannot live without her," he is echoing Admetus's situation, with a very ironic twist in meaning. For both men the sense of loss and the following scenes of recrimination lead to a fairly thorough experience of self-recognition, and after the self-recognition each gets his wife back (for Edward, the recognition and the return have several phases). At the end each play leaves the impression of a successfully continuing marriage, though Eliot has made a major point of study-

---

[12] Pp. 142, 184.

[13] Eliot himself admits that his last act may be only an "epilogue" (*Poetry and Drama*, p. 40). This applies principally to the Celia story, which, being only reported (and the report itself being somewhat inept), comes through as an inadequate counterweight to the Edward-Lavinia comedy. Eliot has not solved, in either *The Family Reunion* or *The Cocktail Party*, the problem of finding a workable dramatic expression of the life of the saint. In this respect *Murder in the Cathedral*, more lyrical and less hampered by the conventions of realism, is more successful. The conception of the saint may require either a more discursive treatment (e.g., that of the novel, as exemplified in Graham Greene's *The Power and the Glory*) or a more concentrated one (e.g., that of the lyric). At the high point both of Eliot's later plays tend to shift from the dramatic to the lyric mode. Partly for this reason, *The Cocktail Party* gives the effect of tragedy manquée, if one may think of tragedy in its essence as the pursuit of spiritual destiny (Edward and Lavinia, it is true, "accept their destiny"—p. 149—but theirs is social and worldly). A student of mine, Dimitir Gotseff, has neatly termed the play "comedy with tragic relief."

ing the impact upon their relationship of the exploration of self
which each participant has undergone, whereas Euripides entirely
excludes consideration of the quality of the postreunion marriage.

While it would be easy to pass over the story of Admetus as simply
another fantasy or popular tale of wonder, as many readers are
probably inclined to do, Eliot has plainly seen that it has great
symbolic possibilities and has modeled on Admetus a character who
embodies a great deal of the ordinary man moving toward middle
age and even of ordinary humanity generally. One can imagine
Eliot consciously refusing to regard Admetus as simply a stock figure
in a romantic drama, replaceable by any other stock figure who
could be called a husband, but instead taking him seriously as a
character and asking, "What kind of man would ask others to die
for him? What is the meaning of the situation that he has worked
himself into?" Perhaps he read Admetus as a precursor of the
Struldbrugs, as an early instance in the tradition of human beings
who want to live forever; for the play makes some inquiry into
the human discontent with the limitations of the human condition.
The man who has fallen out with his fate is "a middle-aged man/
Beginning to know what it is to feel old" and unassured and dis-
enchanted. He is not without intelligence and imagination, but he
is limited in both (Edward speaks of his "dull . . . spirit of mediocrity"). Again, he "has no sense of humour," as Lavinia says of
Edward, who makes a good target for her wit and fails to join
Celia and Lavinia in humorous recognition of their joint plight. He
is given to feeling sorry for himself. When Edward says, "I have
had enough of people being sorry for me," he opens himself up to
Lavinia's riposte, "Yes, because they can never be so sorry for you/
As you are for yourself. And that's hard to bear." He is a self-
deceiver, as is Lavinia; Reilly says to them, "My patients such as
you are the self-deceivers." Edward is vastly self-centered; the phase
of self-discovery which goes on after Lavinia's return is a lamentation on the theme, "Hell is oneself," so painfully carried on that
Lavinia's reply has justice, "Could you bear, for a moment,/To
think about *me?*" To be self-centered is to be lacking in love;
Lavinia says that Edward "has never been in love with anybody."
He lives not understandingly but mechanically; Reilly says that he
is "a set/Of obsolete responses." Edward wants to be "bolstered,
encouraged/ . . . To think well of yourself," as Lavinia sharply
tells him.[14]

[14] The passages quoted in this paragraph are, respectively, on pp. 65, 66, 90,
76, 100, 97, 119, 98, 123, 31, 92.

In all this, Eliot has shrewdly amplified Admetus or actualized
what is latent in him. What is more—and what is not so immediately
apparent—Edward's affair with Celia is certainly to be understood
as a version of Admetus's wanting someone to die for him; in each
case what is at stake is self-esteem, and the heart of the action is a
testing for loyalties and flattering responses. We see this unmistakably in Edward, who comes to realize that Celia has been a psychological utility rather than an object of love; and Eliot's keen analysis of Edward enables us to perceive that Admetus's quest for a
substitute die-er proceeds, not only from obvious love of life, but
also from some self-doubt, some sense of inadequacy to role. Perhaps we might claim as a general truth that excessive love of life
is a function of a feared, or sensed, or actual mediocrity in life.
Admetus, then, cannot be disposed of simply as a ridiculous or
incredible figure. Rather his poll of life-giving alternates, with its
expressionistic immediacy that is initially shocking, exhibits a familiar human need—the need to have reassurance about one's own
significance and power in the world. Wanting an additional life
and wanting an additional love come to much the same thing.
Both heroes are Everyman wrestling with the problem which at
some time in his life he must face—the problem of knowing that
he is not Superman. To Edward one might even apply the familiar
modern term "Little Man." But Eliot neither sentimentalizes nor
idealizes the Little Man; rather he bids him recognize himself,
have no illusions about himself, and come to terms with himself.
Further, he unmistakably generalizes the case of Edward, when he
has him say, "But I am obsessed by the thought of my own in-
significance," as a clear preparation for Reilly's reply:

> Half of the harm that is done in this world
> Is due to people who want to feel important.
> They don't mean to do harm—but the harm does not interest them
> Or they do not see it, or they justify it
> Because they are absorbed in the endless struggle
> To think well of themselves.[15]

A little later Eliot throws us right back into Euripides when he
has Edward say, "I am not afraid of the death of the body,/But this
death is terrifying. The death of the spirit—" [16] Here is the death
theme again, but now with a variation that sums up the present
point. Admetus was afraid of the death of the body, true, but in

[15] Page 111.
[16] Page 113.

his fear we have seen a symbolic expression of a sense of spiritual
inadequacy, the same sense that, at first unrecognized, determined
much of Edward's action. The self-recognition to which Admetus
progressed took, as we have seen, this form: ". . . what then avails
it that I live, if I just live in misery and shame?" Like Admetus,
Edward learns that the real issue is not quantity (of life or love),
but quality of life (i.e., "death of the spirit"). But Euripides, who
has already pushed the satyr drama as far as it will go, cannot go
on to make Admetus act upon his recognition; whereas Edward
must still learn that he cannot prescribe the conditions for the life
of the spirit but must discover, and make do, whatever potentialities
of life lie right there where "death of the spirit" has seemed inevitable.

Edward's mentor, Dr. Reilly, who as "psychiatrist" may seem in-
controvertibly modern, also has his roots in the Euripides play. In
him, indeed, Eliot combines the functions of two characters in
Alcestis—of Heracles, as he has indicated, and, almost as impor-
tantly, of Pheres. Pheres is the source whom we are likely to miss,
because he is easiest to remember as a hurt and bad-tempered father.
But Pheres' abuse of Admetus is not only a response to Admetus's
attack upon him; it is also in part a painfully accurate analysis of
Admetus and in effect a summons to him to see himself as he is:
"You were born to live your own life, whether miserable or for-
tunate; . . . But you . . . you shirked your fate by killing her!
. . . You, the worst of cowards, surpassed by a woman who died
for you . . ." [17] The shock of this denunciation, as well as his own
grief, leads Admetus to face the issue, instead of disguising it by
blaming others and blaming Fate, and to achieve a measure of self-
understanding. As a professional man and as one who is not on the
defensive, Reilly is different from Pheres; but he has the same role
of telling unpleasant truths the shock of which drives Edward (and
later Lavinia) to a new self-recognition. "Resign yourself to be the
fool you are." "You might have ruined three lives/ . . . Now there
are only two—" ". . . you have been making up your case/So to
speak, as you went along." "You were lying to me . . ." [18]

Since Reilly's chief business is helping human beings to see the
truth and find their destiny, it may seem that he is largely explica-
ble as an ingenious version of the angry truth teller, Pheres, and
that his resemblance to Heracles—the only resemblance to which

[17] *Seven Plays*, p. 267.
[18] Pp. 31, 109, 115, 120.

Eliot has publicly called attention—stops at certain incidents of
conduct, such as conviviality in the midst of distress. To this we
might add that Heracles and Reilly both enter the situation at
the right time, both show great power, and both effect rescues—
the one from Death, the other from death of the spirit. But there is
a little more to it than that. Surely to Euripides' audience Heracles
must have been an ambivalent figure—to some a boisterous strong
man, to others a devoted servant of duty, bringing more than brute
force into play. Likewise Reilly can be read as simply an ingenious
psychiatrist, but the more alert will have to see in him something
more. (Incidentally, it is an easy phonetic leap from *Heracles* or
Hercules to *Harcourt-Reilly*.)

Eliot would of course sense the doubleness of Heracles, and it is
difficult to resist the conclusion that he found in him the suggestion
for the thematic basis of his own play—the dualism of world and
spirit, and the interpenetration of world by spirit. For Heracles, as
the son of Alcmena and Zeus, is half human, half divine; and in
Reilly there is an ambiguity which makes a limited naturalistic
view of him seem continually inadequate. Not that Reilly is wholly
"transhumanized," to use the word applied by Julia to the experience undergone by Celia in her "journey"; just as Heracles, in
the words of a recent handbook, "erred occasionally, being half-
mortal," [19] so Reilly "must always take risks," and, as he himself
says, ". . . sometimes I have made the wrong decision." Nor is he
omniscient; Julia reminds him, "You must accept your limitations." [20] But he has remarkable insight and exercises a special
power affecting human destiny. And, although his actions may
virtually all be accounted for in naturalistic terms, Eliot has been
most successful in creating an air, if not of the inexplicable, at
least of the unexplained, of the quizzically irregular, of the modestly
elusive, of the herculean at once urbane and devoted; from the time
when Reilly tells Edward that he (i.e., Edward) has started "a train
of events/Beyond your control," and Lavinia confesses (in terms
that Alcestis might have used), "Yet something, or somebody, compelled me to come," [21] until the end of the play, we are given continual impressions of mysterious forces in action. With his benedic-
tions, Reilly could be the priest; with his emphasis on free will, on

[19] Dan S. Norton and Peters Rushton, *Classical Myths in English Literature*
(New York, 1952), p. 191.
[20] Pp. 146, 185, 148.
[21] Pp. 28 and 94. Cf. similar speeches by Reilly (p. 71) and Lavinia (pp. 86-87).

the choice which is uncompelled but which has its consequences, the theologian; yet in his concern with salvation there is another suggestion that is made most sharply when he says, after dismissing Celia, "It is finished." Since the words on the Cross impose a little more weight than the immediate dramatic situation, which is not primarily an ordeal for Reilly, can bear, we are not wholly comfortable with them here. Yet, as a part of the over-all strategy of suggestion, they enlarge the possibilities before us. For the man who died on the Cross was the "Son of God" but born of a mortal mother—just like Heracles; and the death on the Cross was a mode of bringing life to others, just as Heracles brought back Alcestis from Death, and as Reilly rescues his patients from something which both they and we see as a kind of death. To this extent at least we have another hint of the myth of Christ to which we have already seen parallels in the stories of Alcestis and Celia.

Reilly, it thus becomes clear, is considerably more than the psychiatrist whom in so many details he resembles. He is less the psychological repair man than the soul healer. Psychiatry takes on a spiritual dimension. Out of a couple of interlocking triangles in which the participants are at best half alive come four new lives grounded in the recognition and choice of destiny—that of the artist, that of the ordinary, imperfect, but tolerable and even saving marriage, and that of the saint. These transformations appear as more than standardized "adjustment," as, indeed, the product of great labors by a bringer of life who has both an extraordinary personality and special resources, not wholly identified, to draw upon. The situation which Eliot dramatizes is described with notable accuracy in the final chorus of Euripides, which, in the Aldington translation, even "sounds like" Eliot:

> Spirits have many shapes,
> Many strange things are performed by the Gods.
> The expected does not always happen.
> And God makes a way for the unexpected.
> So ends this action.[22]

[22] Page 286. [The Editor cannot resist appending his own even more Eliotese version of these lines (written in 1952):

> Divinity has many shapes.
> Much is accomplished beyond expectation.
> And for the conceivable no fulfilment:
> For the inconceivable God finds a way.
> Such the event of this action.]

William Arrowsmith: The Turbulence of Euripidean Tragedy

The immediate, salient fact of Euripides' theater is the assumption of a universe devoid of rational order or of an order incomprehensible to men. And the influence of Aristotle is nowhere more obvious than in the fact that this aspect of Euripides' theater is the one least often recognized or acted upon by critics. Yet it is stated both explicitly and implicitly from play to play throughout Euripides' lifetime. "The care of god for us is a great thing," says the chorus of Hippolytus, "if a man believe it. . . . So I have a secret hope of someone, a god, who is wise and plans;/but my hopes grow dim when I see/the actions of men and their destinies./ For fortune always veers and the currents of life are shifting,/ shifting, forever changing course." "O Zeus, what can I say?" cries Talthybius in *Hecuba.* "That you look on men and care? Or do we, holding that the gods exist,/deceive ourselves with unsubstantial dreams/and lies, while random careless chance and change/alone control the world?" Usually desperate, feeble, and skeptical in the first place, it is the fate of these hopes to be destroyed in action. In *Heracles* the fatal chaos of the moral universe is shown formally; a savage reversal which expresses the flaw in the moral universe splits the entire play into two contrasting actions connected only by sequence. Thus the *propter hoc* structure required by Aristotelian drama is in Euripides everywhere annulled by *created* disorder and formal violence. What we get is *dissonance, disparity, rift, peripeteia;* in Euripides a note of firm tonality is almost always the sign of traditional parody; of the false, the unreal, or lost innocence remembered in anguish. What this assumption of disorder means is: first, that form is not organic; second, that character is not destiny, or at best that only a part of it is; and third, that Aristotelian notions of responsibility, tragic flaw, and heroism are not pertinent.

From "*A Greek Theater of Ideas,*" *in* Ideas in the Drama, *ed. John Gassner (New York: Columbia University Press, 1964). Copyright 1964 by Columbia University Press. Reprinted by permission of the publisher.*

The central dissonance assumes a variety of forms. But the commonest is a carefully construed clash between myth (or received reality) on the one hand, and fact (or experienced reality) on the other. Λόγῳ μέν . . . ἔργῳ δέ, as the Greeks put it, contrasting theory (*logos*) and fact (*ergon*), appearance (or pretence) and reality, legend and truth. In *Alcestis,* for instance, Euripides juxtaposes the traditional, magnanimous Admetus with the shabby egotist who results when a "heroic" character is translated into realistic fifth-century terms. By making Alcestis take Admetus at his own estimate, Euripides delays the impact of his central idea—the exposure of Admetus' *logos* by his *ergon*—until the appearance of Pheres, whose savage "realistic" denunciation of his son totally exposes the "heroic" Admetus. By a similar translation, Euripides' Odysseus becomes a demagogue of *real-politik,* Agamemnon a pompous and ineffectual field marshal, and Jason a vulgar adventurer. It was, of course, this technique of realism, this systematic exposure and deflation of traditional heroism, which earned Euripides his reputation for debasing the dignity of the tragic stage. And in some sense the charge is irrefutable. [Euripides' whole bent is clearly anti-traditional and realistic; his sense of rebelliousness is expressed beyond doubt by the consistency with which he rejects religious tradition, by his restless experiments with new forms and new music, and by his obvious and innocent delight in his own virtuosity—his superior psychology and his naturalistic stagecraft. With justifiable pride he might have seen himself as a dramatic pioneer, breaking new ground, and courageously refusing to write the higher parody of his predecessors which his world—and ours—have demanded of him. There must be, I imagine, very few theaters in the world where the man who writes of "people as they are" is automatically judged inferior to the man who writes of "people as they should be."]

. . . First and most significant after the destruction of *propter hoc* structure is the disappearance of the hero. With the sole exception of *Heracles*—Euripides' one attempt to define a new heroism—there is no play which is dominated by the single hero, as is Sophocles' *Oedipus* or *Ajax.*

[Corresponding to the disappearance of the hero is Euripides' "fragmentation" of the major characters. What we get is typically an agon or contest divided between two paired characters (some times there are three): Admetus and Alcestis; Jason and Medea; Hippolytus and Phaedra; Andromache and Hermione; Pentheus and Dionysus, etc] In such a theater, the Aristotelian search for a tragic hero is, of course, meaningless. But the significance of the fragmentation is not easy to assess; it is not enough to say merely that Euripides was temperamentally drawn to such conflict because they afforded him opportunities for psychological analysis. What is striking about the consistently paired antagonists one finds in Euripides is, I think, their obsessional nature. They function like obsessional fragments of a whole human soul: Hippolytus as chastity, Phaedra as sexuality. The wholeness of the old hero is now represented divisively, diffused over several characters; the paired antagonists of the Euripidean stage thus represent both the warring modes of a divided culture and the new incompleteness of the human psyche. Alternatively, as in the *Bacchae,* they embody the principles of conflicting ideas: Pentheus as *nomos,* Dionysus as *physis.*

Richmond Lattimore: An Inverted Tragedy

If we adopt the admittedly somewhat hypothetical scheme according to which tragedy consists in the destruction or self-destruction of an otherwise great man through some fault or flaw in his character, then *Alcestis* might be viewed as a kind of inverted tragedy. For this hero, otherwise no better than ordinary, has one significant *virtue,* which saves him. Thus, again, the progress of the play is from ruin to safety, reversing what might be considered the normal course of tragedy.

From Richmond Lattimore's *Introduction* to his translation of Alcestis, *in* The Complete Greek Tragedies (*Chicago: The University of Chicago Press, 1955*), *III, 4. Copyright 1955 by The University of Chicago Press. Reprinted by permission of the author and publisher.*

Ivan M. Linforth: The Importance of Admetus

Whatever else may be said of the *Alcestis* of Euripides, it is not neglected. Critics do not find it so good that it leaves them speech-

From "*The Husband of Alcestis,*" *in* Queen's Quarterly, *LIII (1946), 147-48. Reprinted by permission of the author and publisher.*

less; readers do not find it so bad that they do not recommend it
to others. Some would be glad to admire the play whole-heartedly
if they had no scruple in their æsthetic conscience; others, not ad-
miring the play themselves, insist that no one else shall admire it.
The charges against the play are those for which Euripides is often
brought to trial. It is uneven, its parts are incongruous, it has no
convincing unity of structure. It contains some exquisite poetry
and some powerful scenes, but the effects are lessened by other
passages which repel the reader. The beauty of Alcestis's sacrifice
is marred by the weak and selfish character of her husband. The
pathos of the scene in which she breathes her last is defiled by the
indecent wrangling of Admetus and Pheres over her dead body.
The decorum of a house of mourning is shattered by the revelry
of Heracles. The reader is not permitted to weep quietly over the
melancholy end of Alcestis. And, finally, when the lamented wife
is restored, he does not feel that either he or the audience should
experience artistic satisfaction.

If the play, *fairly read,* produces these effects, it is certainly not a
good play, and might better be read in excerpts than as a whole.
There are, indeed, some who prefer the fragments of Euripides to
the plays which have survived entire. But the doubt remains
whether the play *is* fairly read. Are not these ugly effects produced
by some distortion in the reader's vision? Is his point of view wrong?
May not the objectionable scenes be quite as important in the poet's
plan as the engrossing scene in which Alcestis holds all eyes and
hearts? May not our disapproval of the play be due to our failure
to perceive what Euripides has actually done?

. . . A study of the comparative values in the play yields results
which may surprise those readers who think almost solely of Alcestis
and wish to forget the scenes which seem to be incongruous. The
simple expedient of counting lines offers a hint that may lead to
the right conclusion. Alcestis speaks only eighty lines, or about
seven per cent of the whole play; Heracles has more than twice as
many, about sixteen per cent; and Admetus has more than Alcestis
and Heracles together, not less than twenty-eight per cent. Alcestis
is present in the orchestra during only one scene of 149 lines (or
twelve per cent of the play), unless we include the passage at the
end where she is mute and passive. Admetus, however, is involved
in the dramatic action from beginning to end, and is present in
the orchestra during sixty per cent of the play. These figures suggest that the mere representation of the death and resurrection of
Alcestis is not the author's chief purpose, and that Alcestis, although

she gives the title to the play and is the chief person in the *story,* is not the principal character in the play.]

A. M. Dale: Rhetoric and Characterization

[Of the characters in this play, Alcestis, Heracles, and Pheres stand out in much more definite outline than Admetus. Their part in the action is limited, and in itself goes a long way to characterize them, while for Alcestis we also have the benefit of description. Selfish father, unselfish wife, gluttonous and heroic son of Zeus: they have to be the sort of people they are or the action would not work. But for Admetus this applies only to his regal hospitality, which affects only a small area of his part in the action. For the rest, Admetus as a person is blown hither and thither by every wind of incident; he is a person to whom things happen] it is his experience that matters, his reactions to what people do or say to him, his *pathos,* not his *ethos.* So far from considering the *Alcestis* a full-length study of *naïveté,* weakness, hysteria, egotism, character-development, and so forth, I do not believe that apart from the ὁσιότης [piety] (10) Euripides had any particular interest in the sort of person Admetus was. The situations in which the plot involves him are too diverse for much personality to appear, or to be intended. For in a well-constructed Euripidean tragedy what controls a succession of situations is not a firmly conceived unity of character but the shape of the whole action, and what determines the development and finesse of each situation is not a desire to paint in the details of a portrait-study but the rhetoric of the situation—what Aristotle calls *dianoia.* Rhetoric is a concept which we tend to hold in some suspicion, as if in its nature there must be something slightly bogus; but we shall never properly understand Greek tragedy unless we realize how closely related were the rhetoric of Athenian life, in the assembly and law-courts and on other public occasions, and the rhetoric of the speeches in drama. Nourished on the psychological novel, we tend to assume that the poet had brooded on the story until the characters took shape in his mind, as if he had asked himself: What would X, being such a man, be likely to say in such a situation? whereas we might sometimes get nearer to the meaning by imagining

From the Introduction to A. M. Dale's edition of Alcestis *(Oxford: The Clarendon Press, 1954), pp. xxvii-xxix. Copyright 1954 by The Clarendon Press. Reprinted by permission of the publisher.*

the question: Suppose a man involved in such a situation, how should he best acquit himself? How gain his point? Move his hearers? Prove his thesis? Convey information lucidly and vividly? The aim of rhetoric is Persuasion, Πειθώ, and the poet is as it were a kind of λογογράφος [speech writer] who promises to do his best for each of his clients in turn as the situations change and succeed one another. This does not by any means exclude an interest in character; the skilful λογογράφος takes that into account in its proper place. But the dominating consideration is: What *points* could be made here? The points may be developed in a set speech, a ῥῆσις, or made and countered in stichomythia. Fertility in arguments, a delight in logical analysis—these are the essentials, though they may be skilfully made to produce an effect of spontaneity. Alcestis has to win her husband's promise never to marry again; her strongest arguments are the magnitude of her own sacrifice and the emotion aroused at the thought of the motherless children and her own death. So like a skilful pleader she makes the most of these things, and sometimes the skill of the pleading obscures the woman Alcestis, as when she emphasizes her own virtue in contrast to the conduct of the parents, or when at the end of the speech she says: "And you, my husband, can boast that you had the noblest of women to wife, and you, my children, that you were born of the noblest of mothers." It is a pleader's peroration, not the spontaneous cry of a noble heart. A modern actress, intent on "being" Alcestis, might well find these lines embarrassing; not so the Greek actor, trained not in "interpretation" but in rhetorical performance, before an audience that expected nothing less. And the dramatist as well as the actor has a technique to which we are unaccustomed. In an earlier scene he has conveyed to us, among other qualities, Alcestis' love for Admetus, which in any case is implicit in the story. But in this scene the action does not require it (it might indeed be a disturbing element), so he omits its expression and leaves only its effect, in her sacrifice; and all the emphasis goes into her anguish for the children. Our presuppositions about dramatic character lead us to expect that such a love will inform her whole utterance everywhere, and so we feel rebuffed. But if we start projecting these feelings into a Euripidean "Portrait of Alcestis," we shall end up with the Alcestis of that delightful modern comedy "The Thracian Horses" who was furious with Heracles for stealing her limelight and chiefly concerned lest she should become famous hereafter as the subject of his Labour number 8(a). It was great fun, but of course it was not Euripides.

Hans Diller: The Role of the House

The vitality of every Euripidean drama depends on its action being placed in a specific milieu without ever losing its relationship to it. A good example is *Alcestis,* the earliest of the extant dramas. Here the house, the royal palace, plays from start to finish a decisive role in the dramatic situation presented by the myth. It is an aristocratic house which has been afflicted by the death of its mistress. We experience the unease of the house before her death and as she dies. Next comes the burial with the painful encounter between father and son in front of the dead woman on her bier, an encounter which effectively destroys the family structure. We watch the return of the lonely widower back to his deserted house. This house which has been afflicted and made desolate by death was in its days of glory a hospitable palace that provided a home even for the gods. The abandoned Admetus, this grandseigneur, keeps up the standing of his house even in the moment of deepest sorrow. He receives Heracles in the guest quarters, which must be left undisturbed by the grief which prevails in the palace close by. The contrast between the desolation of death and the false splendor of hospitality is expressed in the scene between the drunken Heracles and the servant. Finally, by winning back Alcestis, the guest who had been received fills the house once again with life. This renewal of life is only timidly announced, and it seems almost impossible for it to gain mastery again in this house.

From "Umwelt und Masse als dramatische Faktoren bei Euripides," in Euripide, Entretiens sur l'antiquité classique, *Vol. VI, ed. Olivier Reverdin (Geneva: Fondation Hardt pour l'Etude de l'Antiquité Classique, 1960), pp. 91-92. Translated by John R. Wilson. Reprinted by permission of the author and publisher.*

Richmond Lattimore: Hospitality *(Xenia)*

Admetus is drawn to the life, without mercy. He has all the superficial graces and sincerely loves his wife and children, but he lacks

From Richmond Lattimore's Introduction to his translation of Alcestis, in *The Complete Greek Tragedies (Chicago: The University of Chicago Press, 1955), III, 3-4. Copyright 1955 by The University of Chicago Press. Reprinted by permission of the author and the publisher.*

the courage to die as he ought instead of letting his wife die for him; and, further, he lacks the courage to admit, to himself or anyone else, that he ought to be dying but dare not do it. He has, however, one solid virtue. For if he and Alcestis are at last saved not by his own strength and resolution but by Heracles under authority of Apollo, yet there is good reason why these august persons should be so devoted to him. Admetus is the best of friends. The right treatment of guests is a passion, almost an obsession, with him, and in this matter his conviction makes him firm enough to override so great a man as Heracles, with a show of force quite different from his ungrounded violence against Pheres. We may call him hospitable. But if we do, we must understand that, while the lavish entertainment of visitors was a special tradition in Thessaly, the hospitality of Admetus goes far beyond this and is no merely sociable virtue. Rather, this is the old Homeric *xenia*. It is one of the steps by which society progresses from savagery to civilization, when strangers make a willing, immediate, and permanent agreement to be friends. In this sense, *xenia* also includes cases at least of the nonabuse of power against those over whom one has power. Apollo, for punishment, was put at the mercy of Admetus, and Admetus gave him fair and friendly treatment (ll. 8-10; 222-24; 568-79). A different king might have reveled in his power over such a subject and acted outrageously. This is what Laomedon, king of Troy, did to Apollo and Poseidon (*Iliad* xxi. 441-60), and Poseidon never forgave him or his people. So, too, with Heracles, generous hospitality for the tramping hero becomes more than just a matter of correctness or etiquette when one thinks of such "hosts" as Procrustes, Sciron, and Antaeus. Violation of the rights of *xenia* is an underlying theme which directs the action in both the story of Troy and the story of Odysseus. The sin of Laomedon provoked divine rage against Troy; then Paris doomed the city when, after being properly received in the house of Menelaus, he went off with his host's wife and most of his furniture. Decisive for the action of the *Odyssey* is that travesty of *xenia* performed by the suitors when they settle down and make themselves intolerably at home in the house of Odysseus.

Thomas G. Rosenmeyer: A Convention of Greek Tragedy

I have referred to the play as embodying a rhetoric of death. Alcestis is death's chief rhetorician. To begin with, immediately upon her entrance, she intones an address to the Sun, the Clouds, and the Earth (244). As in the first utterance of Prometheus, the apostrophe to the cosmic powers marks her loneliness and her elevation. She is half-abstracted, and the presence of her husband means nothing to her. Then there follows a succession of two scenes whose order is to be explained as a Greek dramatic convention; first the exposition of her passions, in the form of an aria (252), then a set speech voicing her concurrent thoughts (280; cf. the same arrangement later for Admetus, 861, 935). First we behold Alcestis beside herself with the agonies of the vision of death; then abruptly she launches into a reasoned discourse on the meaning and implications of her action. A modern reader will perhaps find this sudden break neither realistic nor aesthetically satisfying. In fact, however, the two scenes are not to be understood as following one another in empirical sequence. They present two sides of one and the same experience which, because of the exigencies of literary formulation, have to be developed independently. Alcestis' response to the fact of death is at least twofold: the prospect engages her passions and her anxiety, but also her reasoning powers. In life, the two modes of reaction are bound together and simultaneous; in writing, they have to be separated unless the author tries to recapture the unity by some surrealistic measures such as those used occasionally by Eugene O'Neill. The Greek method, sanctioned and appreciated, it appears, by the Greek audiences, was to savor each mode by itself, to feature the response of the passions first and the commentary of the intellect second. This is a distortion of what happens in "real life." But to the extent that it catches the total experience more fully than would an emphasis on one or the other of the two modes, the convention may be said to make for a higher kind of realism.

William Arrowsmith: The *Agon*

If we require an idea of the Greek tragic theatre at all, it seems
to me that the clue might best be taken from the very charge of
rhetoric so persistently brought against tragedy, and against Euripides in particular ever since the time of Schlegel. Over and over
again, that is, the late fifth-century tragedy seems to suggest as its
informing image a theatre shaped more by the law-court than by
the altar. In this theatre, the *agon* is viewed essentially as a trial, and
the characters, with all the tricks of sophistic rhetoric, put their
cases in opposed speeches—often of identical length, as though
timed by the water clock of the Athenian dikastery. The audience
in this theatre sits as jurors, not merely a panel of five hundred
jurors, but the full *Heliaea,* the sovereign judicial assembly *(ekkle-
sia).* No appeal, no matter how emotional, is debarred, and each
character in his plea speaks with the formal passion of a man whose
life and fortunes hang upon his words. But it is a formal and
rhetorical passion, below which we can glimpse, as the jury must,
the personal passion and the real motives glozed by the rhetoric
and often exposed in action. Such a theatre, of course, is most appropriate to Euripides, but in some degree, I think, to Sophocles
also, especially in the later plays. I find tentative confirmation of
this not merely in the number of Greek tragedies which openly stage
formal trial scenes, but in the very structure of Euripidean drama:
its persistent avoidance of the single hero in favor of the *agon* of
two chief characters—Pentheus *vs.* Dionysus, Phaedra *vs.* Hippolytus, Orestes *vs.* Menelaus, Ion *vs.* Creusa—and the corresponding
division of so many plays into two almost disparate actions; the flat
assertion of the intention to make a formal plea; and, most important, the constant impression of the plays as problem plays in
which the judgment is never asserted, but left, as it were, to the
audience of jurors. If they understand the play, they make the
right decision, or better, understand that no moral decision is
relevant because the problems are beyond the reach of moral judgment, i.e. are both tragic and true.

*From "The Criticism of Greek Tragedy" by William Arrowsmith, first pub-
lished in the* Tulane Drama Review, *Vol. III, no. iii (T3), Spring 1959. Copyright 1959 by the* Tulane Drama Review, *copyright 1967 by* The Drama Review.
Reprinted by permission of the author and publisher.

Robert B. Heilman: On Beating Death

In later literature there are many works that turn on the dream of beating death. In the English morality play *Everyman* the title character tries to put off, cajole, and even bribe Death (whose rigid integrity makes him as lively a character as Euripides' Death). In Chaucer's *Pardoner's Tale* three young men set out to kill Death. Indefinite postponement is a frequent theme: the Struldbrugs in Swift's *Gulliver's Travels* have managed to live on to an extraordinary age, and Mr. Stoyte in Aldous Huxley's *After Many a Summer Dies the Swan* finds a coarse diet that is supposed to let him reach 150. What all such characters learn is the high cost of living longer: it may be the unforeseen troubles of age, or even an unexpectedly early death, or, as with Admetus, a painful emotional reaction.

From Robert B. Heilman's Introduction to Alistair Elliot's translation of Euripides' Alcestis (San Francisco: Chandler Publishing Company, 1965). Copyright 1965 by Chandler Publishing Company, San Francisco. Reprinted by permission of the publisher.

Kenneth J. Reckford: Charis (Grace) in Eliot and Euripides

Eliot's problem both as a thinker and as a dramatist, which he failed so disastrously to solve in *The Family Reunion* (although not without poetic fireworks of Cassandran imagery), was to establish and visualize a means of communication between the man of spiritual insight and the ordinary people with no particular vocation for martyrdom or any other form of sanctity. This is why *Alcestis* could be a lesson. For if, on the one hand, Euripides made his protagonist into an ordinary man, who gives vent to the various emotions of shock, self-consolation, renewed grief, guilt, and repentance that any husband might feel who had not sufficiently loved his wife while she was alive, Admetus also remains, by a peculiarly

From "Heracles and Mr. Eliot," in Comparative Literature, XVI (1964), 10-11. Copyright 1964 by Comparative Literature. Reprinted by permission of the publisher.

Greek breadth of representation, the head of a royal house, and is
saved as a result of the almost functional openhandedness of his
position. He takes in Heracles by instinct, and his instinct is kingly,
generous, and right.

The spiritual relations in *Alcestis* may be felt behind the powerful
repeated image of *charis,* a "grace" or "favor." *Charis* is refused by
Death to Apollo in the prologue; Alcestis renders it to Admetus, who
promises to be mindful of it; Heracles will "take it as a favor" if Admetus lets him go (but much more, of course, after his entertainment); the parents of Admetus denied it, and Pheres still denies its
value; and finally Heracles returns it to Admetus under ironic cover
of suing for it. The repeated word makes us conscious of a spiritual
bond, which, outwardly expressed in actions of giving and taking,
comes ultimately to unite Alcestis, Admetus, Heracles, and Apollo.
And similarly, in Eliot's play, the give and take of Edward and
Lavinia in their new life suggests their spiritual participation in
that life of grace that earlier united Alex, Julia, and Reilly. We
are still far from Shakespeare's ideally generous community of
"Belmont," where the marriage union of Portia and Bassanio can
become a microcosm of blessed yet everyday Christian behavior.
But we are on the right path.

That aristocratic hospitality was bathed in the grace of attendant
charites, or spirits of giving, would seem more Pindaric than Euripidean; and indeed, Euripides' early *Alcestis* (of 438) is his only
extant play in which this attitude is so happily presented.[1] But
Eliot seems to have been impressed by it, so much so that he came
for the first time to see a possible avenue of redemption in that
seemingly sterile thing, upperclass entertaining. Not only does Edward's abortive cocktail party in Act I bring him in contact with
Reilly-Heracles,[2] but the Chamberlaynes' successful party in Act III
is interpreted correctly by Reilly as their "burden," that is, the
giving of self by which they help atone for the world's wrongs.[3] In
this way they become true "Chamberlaynes." And as their cocktail
party attains its rightful, quasi-sacramental function, so too, by
association with it, does their marriage for the first time approach
being what it was meant to be, "A dignified and commodious sacra-

---

[1] Contrast the more frequent sentiment in later plays, especially *Electra,* that
nobility resides in poor men's houses.

[2] Note also the Biblical implications of "taking in the stranger."

[3] Cf. the lines in *Murder in the Cathedral:*

"This is your share in the eternal burden,
The perpetual glory."

ment." We do not, unfortunately, see Edward and Lavinia dancing around a bonfire. But with almost tragic self-knowledge, and with a curious Eliotic mixture of humor and latent romanticism, they are embarked, like Admetus and Alcestis, on a better life than before. "Oh I'm glad," says Lavinia. "It's begun."

Chronology of Important Dates

B.C. 485-80   Birth of Euripides at Salamis near Athens.

480   Battle of Salamis.

458   Production of Aeschylus' *Oresteia*.

455   Euripides first enters a tetralogy at the Dionysia.

438   *Alcestis*.

431   *Medea*. Outbreak of Peloponnesian War (431-404).

428   *Hippolytus*.

415   *Trojan Women*.

408   *Orestes*. Euripides leaves Athens for the court of Archelaos in Macedonia.

407-6   Death of Euripides in Macedonia.

406-5   Death of Sophocles (born c. 496).

Notes on the Editor and Contributors

JOHN R. WILSON, editor of this volume, is Assistant Professor of Classics at Indiana University and author of articles on Horace, Euripides, and Virgil.

WILLIAM ARROWSMITH, Professor of Classics at the University of Texas, is well known for his translations of Euripides, Aristophanes, and Petronius, as well as for his articles. He is the editor of *The Complete Greek Comedy* (University of Michigan Press, 1961-   ).

HAZEL E. BARNES, Professor of Classics at the University of Colorado, is author of *Humanistic Existentialism: The Literature of Possibility* (1962) and of *Existentialist Ethics* (1967).

D. J. CONACHER is Head of the Department of Classics, Trinity College, University of Toronto, and is the author of numerous articles on Euripides.

The late A. M. DALE (Mrs. T. B. L. Webster) was Professor of Greek at the University of London and is author of *The Lyric Metres of Greek Drama* (1948) and editor of Euripides' *Helen* (1967).

HANS DILLER, Professor of Classical Philology at the University of Kiel, is the author of many articles on Greek tragedy.

KURT VON FRITZ, Professor of Classical Philology at the University of Munich (and formerly Professor at Columbia University), is the author of *Pythagorean Politics in Southern Italy* (1940) and *The Theory of the Mixed Constitution in Antiquity* (1958).

ROBERT B. HEILMAN, Chairman of the Department of English at the University of Washington, is author of *This Great Stage: Image and Structure in King Lear* (1948) and *Magic in the Web: Action and Language in Othello* (1956).

D. M. JONES, Professor of Greek at the University of London, is a contributor of numerous articles to classical and linguistic journals.

IVAN M. LINFORTH, Professor Emeritus of Greek at the University of California at Berkeley, is the author of *Solon the Athenian* (1919), *The Arts of Orpheus* (1951), and a number of long papers on Sophocles in *University of California Studies in Classical Philology*.

RICHMOND LATTIMORE, Professor of Greek at Bryn Mawr, is co-editor and part translator of *The Complete Greek Tragedies,* translator of Homer, Pindar, and Greek lyrics, a poet in his own right, and author of *The*

Poetry of Greek Tragedy (1958) and *Story Patterns in Greek Tragedy* (1964).

KENNETH J. RECKFORD is Associate Professor of Classics at the University of North Carolina and is author of articles on Persius, Horace, Homer, and Menander.

THOMAS G. ROSENMEYER, Professor of Greek and Comparative Literature at the University of California at Berkeley, is co-author of *The Meters of Greek and Latin Poetry* (1963) and translator of Bruno Snell's *The Discovery of the Mind*.

WESLEY D. SMITH, Associate Professor of Classics at the University of Pennsylvania, has written articles on Euripides' *Hippolytus, Suppliants,* and *Orestes.*

ERNA P. TRAMMELL is also author of "The Grave of Neoptolemos" (*The Classical Journal* XLIV [1949], 270 f.).

Selected Bibliography

The works by Arrowsmith, Conacher, Dale, Linforth, Reckford, and Rosenmeyer which are here reproduced only in part can all be profitably consulted in their entirety. For those who read German, Kurt von Fritz's essay is particularly enlightening in its comparative study of later versions of *Alcestis*.

General Books on Euripides

Gilbert Murray. *Euripides and His Age*. New York and London, 1913 (paperback edition with introduction by H. D. F. Kitto, London, 1965). Still the most lively general introduction to Euripides.

G. M. A. Grube. *The Drama of Euripides*. London, 1941. A sensible book, with some valuable introductory chapters on problems that face the modern reader of Euripides.

F. L. Lucas. *Euripides and His Influence*. Boston, 1923. Useful for its full account of Euripides' influence.

Extracts from Books

H. D. F. Kitto. *Greek Tragedy: A Literary Study*. 3rd edition, London, 1961, pp. 187-381. Always fresh and challenging.

Richmond Lattimore. *Story Patterns in Greek Tragedy*. Ann Arbor and Toronto, 1964, pp. 60-64, 70-71. The suppression of inconvenient mythological data. The dramatic ceremonial at the ending of *Alcestis*.

Bruno Snell. *Poetry and Society*. Bloomington, Ind., 1961, pp. 82-86. The spiritual as opposed to the practical concept of marriage in *Alcestis*.

Articles

J. T. Sheppard. "Admetus, Verrall, and Professor Myres," *Journal of Hellenic Studies*, XXXIX (1919), 37-47. Especially good on the conventional values represented by the characters in the play.

Anne Pippin Burnett. "The Virtues of Admetus," *Classical Philology,* LX (1965), 240-55 (also reprinted in the Twentieth Century Views volume, *Euripides,* ed. Erich Segal, Prentice-Hall, Inc., 1968). The most ingenious of the whole-hearted defenses of Admetus.

William Arrowsmith is preparing an article on *Alcestis* for a forthcoming issue of *Arion.*

Translations

Richmond Lattimore, translator, in *The Complete Greek Tragedy* (Chicago, 1955, now available in many editions).

Philip Vellacott, translator, in *Euripides: Three Plays.* Penguin Classics, Harmondsworth, 1953. Sometimes better than Lattimore in its spareness, but generally inferior.

TWENTIETH CENTURY
INTERPRETATIONS
MAYNARD MACK, *Series Editor*
Yale University

NOW AVAILABLE
Collections of Critical Essays
ON

ADVENTURES OF HUCKLEBERRY FINN
ALL FOR LOVE
ARROWSMITH
AS YOU LIKE IT
THE BOOK OF JOB
THE CASTLE
THE DUCHESS OF MALFI
EURIPIDES' ALCESTIS
THE FROGS
SIR GAWAIN AND THE GREEN KNIGHT
GRAY'S ELEGY
THE GREAT GATSBY
GULLIVER'S TRAVELS
HAMLET
HENRY IV, PART TWO
HENRY V
THE ICEMAN COMETH
JULIUS CAESAR
KEATS'S ODES
OEDIPUS REX
THE PORTRAIT OF A LADY
A PORTRAIT OF THE ARTIST AS A YOUNG MAN

Samson Agonistes
The Scarlet Letter
The Sound and the Fury
Tom Jones
Twelfth Night
Utopia
Walden
The Waste Land
Wuthering Heights